Gorbachev and the Decline of Ideology in Soviet Foreign Policy

Gorbachev and the Decline of Ideology in Soviet Foreign Policy

Sylvia Woodby

Westview Press
BOULDER, SAN FRANCISCO, & LONDON

Westview Special Studies on the Soviet Union and Eastern Europe

The views expressed in this book are those of the author only and do not necessarily represent those of the Department of State.

This Westview softcover edition is printed on acid-free paper and bound in library-quality, coated covers that carry the highest rating of the National Association of State Textbook Administrators, in consultation with the Association of American Publishers and the Book Manufacturers' Institute.

All rights reserved. No part of this publication may be reproduced or transmitted in any form or by any means, electronic or mechanical, including photocopy, recording, or any information storage and retrieval system, without permission in writing from the publisher.

Copyright © 1989 by Westview Press, Inc.

Published in 1989 in the United States of America by Westview Press, Inc., 5500 Central Avenue, Boulder, Colorado 80301, and in the United Kingdom by Westview Press, Inc., 13 Brunswick Centre, London WC1N 1AF, England

Library of Congress Cataloging-in-Publication Data
Woodby, Sylvia.
  Gorbachev and the decline of ideology in Soviet foreign policy / Sylvia Woodby.
    p. cm.—(Westview special studies on the Soviet Union and Eastern Europe)
  Includes bibliographical references.
  ISBN 0-8133-7783-8
  1. Soviet Union—Foreign relations—1985– . 2. Gorbachev, Mikhail Sergeevich, 1931– . 3. Perestroika. 4. Communism—Soviet Union. I. Title. II. Series.
DK289.W66 1989
327.47—dc20
                                                                             89-24769
                                                                                CIP

Printed and bound in the United States of America

∞   The paper used in this publication meets the requirements of the American National Standard for Permanence of Paper for Printed Library Materials Z39.48-1984.

10 9 8 7 6 5 4 3 2 1

Contents

PART ONE
EVOLUTION OF GORBACHEV'S NEW VISION

Introduction   3

Ideology and *Perestroika*   5

    The Domestic Agenda, 5
    Ideology as an Obstacle to Reform, 7
    Ideological Revision as a Tool of Reform, 9

Ideology and Foreign Policy   14

    The Foreign Policy Agenda, 14
    Ideology as an Obstacle to Reform, 16
    Ideological Revision as a Tool of Reform, 18

Banishing the Class Struggle   24

    Peaceful Coexistence and the Priority
        of Human Values, 26
    New Views of the Class Enemy, 28
    Orthodox Challenges, 30

Foreign Policy Self-Criticism   35

    Errors of the Past, 35
    Improving the Quality of Foreign Policy
        Decision-making, 38

Ideological Revision and Gorbachev's
Foreign Policy Goals   40

Security Policy, 40
Regional Conflicts, 46
Self-Image and Imperial Presence, 49

Prospects for Gorbachev's Secular Outlook 54

Notes 62

PART TWO
SELECTIONS FROM RELEVANT SPEECHES AND DOCUMENTS

1. Political Report of the CPSU Central Committee to the 27th Congress of the Communist Party of the Soviet Union, *Mikhail Gorbachev* (February 1986) 75

2. 70th Revolutionary Anniversary Speech, *Mikhail Gorbachev* (November 1987) 81

3. Speech to a Meeting of Representatives of Parties and Movements Participating in the Revolutionary Anniversary Celebrations, *Mikhail Gorbachev* (November 1987) 86

4. Speech to the Central Committee Plenum, *Mikhail Gorbachev* (February 1988) 89

5. "I Cannot Waive Principles," *Nina Andreyeva* (March 1988) 93

6. "Principles of Restructuring: Revolutionary Nature of Thinking and Acting," *Pravda* (April 1988) 96

7. Thesis No. 10, Issued by the Central Committee for the 19th All-Union Party Conference, *Pravda* (May 1988) 100

8. Report of the Central Committee to the 19th All-Union Party Conference, *Mikhail Gorbachev* (June 1988)	103
9. Speech to the United Nations General Assembly, *Mikhail Gorbachev* (December 1988)	109
10. Speech to Kiev Workers, *Mikhail Gorbachev* (February 1989)	115
11. Report to the Congress of People's Deputies, *Mikhail Gorbachev* (May 1989)	118
Index	121

PART ONE

Evolution of Gorbachev's New Vision

Introduction

Dramatic and controversial changes are taking place in the Soviet Union; changes in the ideology of foreign policy are among the most dramatic and controversial. Through a combination of actions and words, Mikhail Gorbachev has sought to convince the West that the USSR is not dangerous, either militarily or politically. At home, he has sought to convince his countrymen that it is time to abandon the idea that the USSR is at war with the non-socialist world, and that it must keep the West at arms length. Instead, Gorbachev has declared his readiness to make concessions to secure stable East-West relations which will permit the USSR to promote its own interests more effectively, and to concentrate on ambitious and urgent domestic reforms.

To promote this approach, Gorbachev has rejected long-accepted ideologically based views of the world and the Soviet Union's place in it. Specifically, Gorbachev has said ideology should be removed from interstate relations altogether, and Soviet foreign policy priorities reordered accordingly. This means giving up the idea that East-West conflict is the central dynamic, and the notion that world politics is dominated by fundamental, irreconcilable hostility between pro-capitalist and pro-communist states. Gorbachev essentially argues that a conflict model of world politics may have been appropriate in the past, but no longer serves Soviet national interests.

In ideological matters Gorbachev is an iconoclast; that is, he seems most interested in ridding himself of constraints related to habitual and doctrinally sanctified approaches. His attacks on ideology have supported his efforts to change established ways of doing things, to innovate and experiment. At home, Gorbachev insists he is searching for better methods of achieving socialist values, even as he proposes to discard many institutions and practices which have been accepted as "socialist" for a very long time. In foreign policy, Gorbachev blames ideological values and ideological thinking for conflict. Thus he advocates that ideological values be subordinated to efforts to secure a less threatening environment.

Gorbachev's secular view of the world is both novel and familiar. Shifts in Soviet thinking about foreign policy have occurred before, and have not always proved lasting. Moreover, many in the West are skeptical or apprehensive about taking Soviet professions of peaceful intent at face value. At the same time, the changes in the style and tone of Soviet foreign policy are so remarkable and the official attitude toward the ideology of foreign policy so unusual that a closer inspection is warranted. Without attempting a full analysis of current Soviet policies, Part One will the examine the ways in which Gorbachev has modified the ideology of foreign policy, and offer a tentative assessment of the prospects and potential impact of these changes. Extracts from Gorbachev's own speeches and relevant documents make up Part Two.

Ideology and *Perestroika*

Revisions in the ideology of Soviet foreign policy parallel those which have accompanied domestic political reforms, and are linked with them both explicitly and implicitly. A brief outline of Gorbachev's domestic political agenda will help to show why.

The Domestic Agenda

As soon has he was selected as General Secretary, Mikhail Gorbachev made clear that he was to be an agent of reform. He was willing to speak plainly about the problems and weaknesses of the economy, and to acknowledge major defects in performance. But his appreciation of the scale of the problem, the depth of his criticism and the boldness of his recommendations for changes have grown over his time in office. Gorbachev began with complaints that the Soviet system was not performing up to its potential, despite many successes. Greater productivity, improved management and better work discipline were necessary, he said, to overcome "unfavorable trends" and "difficulties" in order to improve both economic growth and the lot of the average citizen.[1] Thus he initially described his program as a call for intensive development to accelerate Soviet growth by raising productivity, a program which he said could have "relatively quick results."[2] But as Gorbachev's assessment of the size of the problem grew, his view of the Soviet system became increasingly negative and his optimism faded. By the 27th Party Congress in February, 1986, Gorbachev was very sharply critical of the corruption and inertia of the Brezhnev period (now called the years of *zastoi*, or stagnation). Gorbachev attacked those who clung to old ideas and resisted change; he demanded bold actions, creativity and innovation to modernize and restructure the economic system.[3] In 1987, Gorbachev characterized the Soviet economy as in a "pre-crisis stage," and called for radical reform in all areas. He has cited failures in every area of social and economic performance, for which he blames over-bureaucratization, poor management, bad work habits, and corruption.

As the results and the pace of this "restructuring" (*perestroika*) have proved disappointing, Gorbachev sought to mobilize support by ever more alarming revelations about the defects of the Soviet economy. In a February 1988 report to the Central Committee, Gorbachev declared that excluding oil and alcohol production, there had actually been no economic growth in the USSR for the last two decades.[4] The Central Committee has declared that Brezhnev's leadership "brought the country to the brink of economic crisis. . . . The growth of production, its efficiency, and the improvement of the population's living standard came to a halt."[5] In hammering home the idea that a "Leninist revival" of the Soviet Union was required, Gorbachev delivered a sad but damning indictment of the whole system:

> Throughout the last 70 years our party and people have been inspired by the ideas of socialism and have been building it. But by virtue of both external and internal factors we were unable to realize sufficiently fully the Leninist principles of the new social system. This was seriously hampered by the personality cult, the administrative decree system of management which grew up in the thirties, bureaucratic, dogmatic and voluntarist distortions, tyranny, and in the late seventies and early eighties lack of initiative and retarding phenomena leading to stagnation.[6]

While Gorbachev has backed off from a complete repudiation of established ways of doing things, the sum of his changes mean a sharp reversal of past practices. He has proposed decentralizing the organization of the economy, enforcing profitability accounting and self-financing on enterprises, encouraging cooperatives, leasing land to family farming groups, and permitting individual enterprises to conclude trade and investment agreements with foreigners. Wholesale trade, price reform, and market mechanisms (perhaps even a convertible ruble) are in the works.

Intellectual and cultural life are in ferment, for Gorbachev has insisted on a policy of *glasnost'* (openness) to stimulate creative thinking, air problems and help activate public participation in the reform process. Restrictions on cultural life have been eased, stimulating a flood of controversial plays, music and publications. The press is increasingly contentious, and now covers many issues and types of events formerly prohibited. Gorbachev has also begun to reform the political system. Asserting that "democratization" is essential to the renaissance of Soviet society, he has called for greater popular involvement in managing public affairs at all levels. This has meant new rules for party and state elections (secret ballot, multiple candidacies, and runoffs), moves to reduce the Party's role in the day-to-day management of the economy, and redesigned political institutions to enhance the role of the legislature and the head of state. The special 19th Party conference held in the summer of 1988 endorsed most of Gorbachev's proposals for institutional reform, and produced an important compromise which provides that local party bosses will be nominated to head local government bodies. A Congress of People's Deputies was selected in April 1989 through a complicated new system of contested elections in which a number of important Party officials and military figures were rejected by the voters. This new Congress in turn elected a refurbished Supreme Soviet.

While Gorbachev's economic reform has promised much, the results so far are not encouraging. Cuts in alcohol production have stimulated home distilling and led to sugar rationing. Food shortages are still serious, and the switch to new economic management principles has meant some categories of consumer goods are simply not available. Democratization and openness may have been meant to facilitate the promotion of new ideas and replacement of opponents, but the climate of change has encouraged reformers, critics and discontented all over the socialist camp. Soviet troops have been sent to quell ethnic violence between Armenians and Azerbaijanis, and to suppress nationalist demonstrations in Georgia. Communal violence and disorders have erupted in Uzbekistan. The Baltic peoples have voiced complaints about their status and formed movements which demand economic autonomy and raise the possibility of secession from the USSR. Czechs have demonstrated against the 1968 Soviet invasion, strikes in Poland brought down the Cabinet and paved the way for a noncommunist Premier, and a new Hungarian leadership has discussed a multiparty system.

Despite all acknowledged difficulties, Gorbachev continues aggressively to defend his program and rally supporters, insisting that there is no alternative to radical reform. He has also taken steps to consolidate himself politically by becoming head of state, purging the Central Committee and promoting like-minded associates to key positions.[7]

Ideology as an Obstacle to Reform

Gorbachev's ideological message is essentially a negative one. That is, he regards ideology as an obstacle if it means that old doctrines might be used to defend the status quo against the changes he seeks. To the extent that ideology interferes with his reform program, ideology is the enemy. "Notions that have become established, and in particular, prejudices," Gorbachev has declared, "should not stop us here."[8]

Gorbachev's criticisms of ideology make it clear that he is impatient with those who would use it to resist his reforms. He has identified two practical problems that are ideologically based. One is dogmatism—that is, the tendency to reject all new ideas and defend established ideas as inflexible truths. The other is a "command mode" of decision making by party leaders at all levels who assume they are infallible and suppress discussion and criticism. According to Gorbachev, these assumptions perpetuate mistakes and prevent the kind of self-scrutiny that could inspire change. His remarks about ideology are unkind: he has ridiculed "grandiloquent twaddle"[9] and "scholastic theorization."[10] He has also complained that for some people, "any change in the economic mechanism is seen to entail a virtual departure from socialist principles,"[11] and has linked the success of his reforms to the abolition of "hollow verbiage and didacticism."[12]

Gorbachev prefers realism and pragmatism—a philosophy of means—and repeatedly urges that "ideological work be brought closer to life". He insists that realism and pragmatism are Leninist. Thus Gorbachev has reminded Soviets that Lenin would want them "to make a profound study of realities, to assess social phenomena realistically, from class positions, and to be in a constant creative quest for the best ways of implementing the ideals of communism."[13]

Like other Soviet reformers, Gorbachev prefers "flexible" and "creative" Marxism-Leninism.

> Any attempt to turn the theory by which we are guided into an assortment of ossified schemes and prescriptions valid everywhere and in all contingencies is most definitely contrary to the essence and spirit of Marxism-Leninism.[14]

Thus it was wrong to turn Lenin's ideas into dogma and "ossified social thought,"[15] permitting impractical and unrealistic people to cling to old methods which are no longer working.

Gorbachev has also helped to clear the field for *perestroika* by his attacks on the Soviet past. He has called for a critical review of Soviet history to learn how to correct mistakes and overcome "deviations," "distortions" and "errors."[16] Cancellation of school history examinations in the spring of 1988 was symbolic of the new mood in the USSR—nothing is sacrosanct except the need for reform. (The historian Afanasyev recently complained that "there is no country in the world in which history has been so falsified as ours," and demanded that history be "de-ideologized."[17]) Gorbachev apparently is convinced that permitting all established institutions, policies and practices to be questioned is a prerequisite for the kind of changes that are necessary,

Ideology and Perestroika

and has marshalled quotations in which Lenin criticizes those who merely memorize ideological formulas[18] and are unable to change with the times.[19]

Ideological Revision as a Tool of Reform

Gorbachev's first priority was to reduce the force of the ideology as a bar to change in general; a second has been to use the ideology to justify the particular new ideas, policies and kinds of reinterpretations he advocates. Gorbachev insists he is a good Leninist, and assertions abound that the reform program is completely in conformity with Leninism. *Perestroika* has been justified by citing a Lenin comment on the possibility that a socialist government might have to make several different attempts at socialism. Gorbachev has also used Lenin's writings and pronouncements of the NEP (New Economic Policy) period as proof not only that Lenin was willing to radically revise his recommended policies, but also that Lenin approved of market mechanisms and cooperatives, and was hostile to bureaucratized management.[20]

In April 1988, a summary of Leninism by Razumovsky (the 1988 Lenin birthday speech) stated boldly that "restructuring has brought us closer to Lenin, and Lenin to us." The theory and practice of *perestroika* "are organically merged with the ideas and practice of Leninism." This makes Lenin's ideas the "starting point" of *perestroika*: "The ideology of renewal represents a development and enrichment of Leninist views of socialism and its historic mission in radically changed conditions."[21]

On balance, Gorbachev's critique is primarily aimed at the principles and practices which are institutionalized in the mechanisms of the centrally planned economy. He has sought to dissociate these mechanisms and procedures from Lenin. Instead, he credits Stalin and others with devising an "administrative command" system which seemed appropriate for a period of rapid industrialization, but no longer works.[22] Vadim Medvedev, the Politburo member who is Chairman of the Central Committee Commission on Ideology, has summarized this view as follows:

> Faithfulness to Leninism in words alone, surrounded by arbitrarily selected quotations, not only failed to be backed up by real deeds, but on the contrary, was accompanied by profound and grave distortions of Leninist principles in the spirit of barracks-room socialism, the imposition and establishment of an administrative command system, arbitrariness, lawlessness, depreciation of man, and hackneyed oversimplification of the

idea of a direct transition to higher forms of production and social organization.

We inevitably bear in mind that Vladimir Ilich's own views were constantly developing, and underwent an important evolution in the transition from war communism to the New Economic Policy. This is now being very seriously studied and analyzed.

Today it is no longer enough to simply return to the Leninist concept of socialism. The main difficulty is to interpret Leninist ideas in light of contemporary conditions, contemporary experience, and contemporary tasks, and in the general context of contemporary world development and the present stage of civilization.[23]

If the principles, institutions and practices of the Soviet state represent the product of incorrect or distorted "interpretations" or "applications" of Marxism-Leninism, then they may be justly discarded for new ones.

What kinds of interpretations does Gorbachev seek? Gorbachev's Leninism is strongly pragmatic, and thus permissive. He has made success the test of orthodoxy, and has described a pragmatic search for solutions to "real-life problems" as the major responsibility of ideological work. Efficacy and performance count most: "The chief performance criteria now are dynamic rates of economic growth, high efficiency indicators, and palpable positive changes in the social sphere. We will be judged by the visible changes in our society, by the practical results." As Gorbachev has said, "we are for everything that promotes socialism, and against everything that does not."[24]

Two of the most striking examples of ideologically sensitive change are the promotion of cooperatives, and the leasing of farmland to family groups. Gorbachev denies that these policies promote private property. He justifies both on pragmatic grounds, since they are designed to increase the productivity of the Soviet economy. The role of incentives has figured prominently in Gorbachev's discussion of reform strategies. He insists that using personal interest to increase production is a "Leninist precept," and has praised "unfettered human initiative" and economic competition as public policy tools:

> The chief question in the theory and practice of socialism is how, on a socialist basis, to create more powerful stimuli than under capitalism for economic, scientific, technical and social progress, how to most efficiently combine planned leadership with the interests of the individual and of the collective. This is a most complex question the answer to which has been sought and is being sought by socialist thought and by social practice. At the present stage of socialism the significance of this question is increasing immeasurably. . . . It is theoretically and practically indisput-

able that the interest of the working people as masters of production is the strongest interest, the most powerful driving force for the acceleration of socioeconomic, scientific and technical progress.[25]

Gorbachev has also enlivened discussions of social policy by adopting the notion that Soviet society is not homogeneous, but riddled with antagonistic interests whose conflicts must be carefully managed. He has repeatedly attacked the notion that social justice means egalitarianism, and blamed "levelling" prejudices for the slow progress of many reforms.[26] This problem has apparently been most acute in the countryside, where Gorbachev has said that property relations must change so that the peasant can be "master of the land:"

> Promoting lease-based relations in the country is one of the most important and, probably, most decisive ways at this stage to restructure socialist ownership relations. It is through lease-holding that it is possible to implement in full Lenin's idea of drawing on personal interest, restoring the sense of being one's own master, and encouraging creative possibilities.[27]

Characteristically, Gorbachev asserts that "no stereotypes or dogmas must stand in the way of resolving the food problem."[28]

By promoting the ideological acceptability of performance criteria, Gorbachev clears the way for a great deal of creativity and innovation, but raises understandable questions about his standards. Gorbachev is sensitive to this problem. He emphasizes the need to find "new approaches, new methods and new discoveries" which can free socialism "from everything that is pseudosocialist," but at the same time insists that *perestroika* should continue "within the framework of the socialist choice."[29] He has been a little vague on how to distinguish the bad from the good, and has actually said that "real work needed to be done" to clarify the criteria for judging whether something is or is not socialist.

In February, 1988, Gorbachev confronted the ideological problem directly in a speech to a Central Committee plenum which acknowledged that "an acute struggle" about his reforms was underway. He noted that because of the scope of *perestroika*, "some people are confused, wondering whether we are backsliding from socialist positions . . . and whether we are not revising Marxist-Leninist teaching itself." Gorbachev insisted, however, that his reforms amount to a "revival of the Leninist nature" of the system:

> Restructuring obliges us to take a new look at certain familiar characteristics and contrast not only the route we have traveled but the route

still to come with the criteria of progress and the goals for building the new society formulated in the classics of Marxism-Leninism. In other words, to verify the direction of our practical actions against the main beacons which have guided communists for more than a century now, and not simply to repeat parroted truisms for the sake of some kind of ritual, but to seek answers to the many issues generated by the prevailing situation.

That, comrades, is why the problems of ideological activity and the questions of the theory of socialism and restructuring are of such great importance.[30]

At the 19th Party Conference in June, 1988, Gorbachev acknowledged the need for "constructive and positive reference points to show the way and the means to bring practice closer to the ultimate aims and ideals of socialism." Accordingly, he offered a list of seven basic features of a socialist society:

- A society dedicated to human development.
- A society with an efficient and dynamic economy.
- A planned economy permitting producers broad independence within a market, comprising varied forms of public and personal property which ensure that working people control production, and rewarding each according to his work.
- A system of social justice without egalitarianism or exploitation.
- A highly cultured and moral system based on popular sovereignty.
- A society of democratic management and interethnic harmony.
- A system with a peaceful and civilized foreign policy respecting the choices of other peoples.

He offered this list of "objective criteria of the socialist spirit" to prove that his reforms were not eroding basic socialist values.[31]

Nonetheless, his pragmatism, his attacks on established institutions and procedures, and the delays in attempting to clarify the values and goals of his reforms have made Gorbachev vulnerable to charges that he is without direction. In early 1989, Gorbachev warned Soviet citizens against falling into "panic, pessimism, despondency." The "tumultuous process" of *perestroika*, he said, has "thrown some people off balance and confused them." This accounted for charges that the reforms were "all but deviating from socialist principles and ideals," "all but surrendering the positions of socialism in the economy," and so forth. He decisively rejected any claims that socialism had failed, and criticized a lack of faith in our "historical choice." Offering a frank review of the mixed record of *perestroika* to date, Gorbachev noted that some longed for the "good old days" and a firm hand at the center, others were doubting the ability of the system to reform itself, and some were attacking the party. Nonetheless he defended *perestroika* despite its difficulties and denied that his government was "blundering in the dark."

> Assertions that we have no strategy or policy of restructuring are groundless. . . . I think we ought to reject all the speculation that we supposedly have no idea where we are heading and what we are doing, and all of us ought to become actively involved in the further intensification and interpretation of restructuring, and in the construction work to put the plans mapped out into practice.[32]

However ardently Gorbachev claims to be a proponent of basic socialist values, socialist values may not be the issue. The reforms demand "a sharp break with an entire way of life, with customs and notions that have developed over many decades,"[33] and are thus inherently threatening in the short term, whatever their ultimate social effect.

Ultimately, Gorbachev's argument is apocalyptic: the Soviet system must find new ways to promote socialist values more effectively, or fail—and destroy socialism's reputation for good:

> We are confronted with a stark alternative. Either we continue moving down the old, much travelled track—toward even greater stagnation and the economic, social, and even political dead end with the ensuing risk of being pushed to the sidelines of progress, or we embark on an arduous but vitally important path of our society's revolutionary renewal, of imparting to socialism a new qualitative dimension that would meet the highest standards of humanism and progress. . . .
>
> We understand well that both the international prestige of socialism and its impact on world processes will depend in many ways on how this works out in our country. I would say we are simply doomed to the success of restructuring because we have no right to allow a different outcome.[34]

Gorbachev's innovations challenge the old canons of applied Marxism-Leninism; whether Gorbachev's ideas will replace them will depend both on the practical results of his new policies and the success of the efforts to redefine the social meaning of Marxist-Leninist values.

Ideology and Foreign Policy

While Gorbachev has been an active diplomat, he has been an ardent proponent of the view that foreign policy should serve domestic needs. Gorbachev very early indicated that his ambitious domestic program called for a "calm" international atmosphere to permit concentrating attention and resources on domestic reform.[35] Thus he has said that Soviet diplomacy should "create the best possible foreign conditions for accelerating the socioeconomic development of Soviet society."[36] At the same time, it was clear that Gorbachev considered East-West tension to be a major obstacle to his reforms. Gorbachev also inherited many foreign policy problems. His first statements about the need for new approaches made it evident he was seeking a way out of some bad situations: Soviet efforts to sow discord in NATO and disrupt the American deployment of intermediate nuclear forces in Europe had failed, and the Soviet walkout from the arms control talks on both strategic and intermediate forces had accomplished nothing. In the meantime, the U.S. military build-up was continuing, and American military aid was reaching insurgencies against embattled Marxist regimes in Angola, Kampuchea, Nicaragua and Afghanistan.

The Foreign Policy Agenda

Gorbachev and other Soviet spokesmen have been quite open about their desire to change their image and retake the initiative in international relations. Speaking to the Ministry of Foreign Affairs in May 1986, Gorbachev emphasized the importance of initiative, of "energetic steps to get rid of the stereotypes and cliches of the past," and "truly dynamic, effective, combative diplomacy." He called upon his diplomats to overcome inertia and the kind of "senseless stubbornness" which had earned Soviet negotiators the title of "Mister Nyet," and advised them to act boldly to try new approaches to the European Economic Community, arms control negotiations, human rights issues and security problems in Asia. He also stressed the need to find ways for the USSR to enter the world economy.[37] Foreign Minister Eduard Shevardnadze has also reproached Soviet diplomats for being out of touch with real national interests, and therefore for contributing to the steady loss of the USSR's status, and the backwardness of its power. "Beyond the borders of the Soviet Union," he said, "you and I represent a great country which in the last fifteen years has been steadily losing its position as one of the leading industrially developed countries." Now, he said, "we must try to reach a situation where interrelations among states encumber our economy as little as possible and create a stable psychological atmosphere in which Soviet people can work peacefully."[38] Indeed, Gorbachev and Shevardnadze have undertaken to improve Soviet relations with the West European countries, but also with Japan, the ASEAN (Association of Southeast Asian Nations) states, and a number of Latin American governments. Soviet Asian initiatives intended to mend relations with China included some concessions on the border dispute, an announced withdrawal of Soviet troops from Mongolia and support for a Vietnamese withdrawal from Kampuchea. The Soviet Union has even moved toward ties with long-alienated countries such as Israel and South Korea.

Reducing East-West tensions has been a central objective. Active Soviet diplomacy, a new multilateralism, a willingness to make concessions have helped to produce a dramatic improvement in Soviet relations with Western countries. Soviet acceptance of on-site verification and readiness to eliminate all their intermediate range nuclear missiles reinvigorated the U.S.-Soviet arms control negotiations, and led to the Intermediate Nuclear Forces (INF) treaty of December, 1987. A new forum for conventional force reduction discussions between the NATO and Warsaw Pact countries has opened in Vienna (the Conventional Forces in Europe talks, or CFE). Discussions began in a favorable atmosphere following Gorbachev's December 1988 announcement of unilateral cuts in Soviet armed forces and military spending. The USSR has paid its United Nations dues and promoted multilateral diplomatic solutions for regional conflicts. Soviet troop withdrawals from Afghanistan which began in early 1988 were completed in 1989 in accordance with an agreement facilitated by UN officials. Gorbachev has also supported a UN-brokered settlement in the Iran-Iraq war, and a U.S.-mediated agreement for Namibian independence linked to a withdrawal of Cuban troops from Angola. Joint ventures between Soviet enterprises and foreign investors are now encouraged, as is greater Soviet participation in existing international economic institutions. Jamming of foreign radio broadcasts into the Soviet Union has ceased, restrictions on travel to and from the USSR have been eased, prominent dissidents have been released, and churches opened. Gorbachev has aggressively promoted discussions with the West on human rights issues, and offered

Moscow as a site for an international conference on human rights in 1991.

Ideology as an Obstacle to Reform

Gorbachev's approach to foreign policy has broken with many old traditions. In a pattern which follows his domestic policy, Gorbachev has used apocalyptic imagery about the need for "revolutionary" shifts in thought and action, and has criticized ideological dogmatism in foreign policy almost as frequently as he has for domestic policy. Instead, Gorbachev demands "new political thinking" in foreign affairs.

> Changes in current world affairs are so deep-going and significant that they require the reassessment and comprehensive analysis of all factors. The situation created by nuclear confrontation calls for new approaches, methods and forms of relations between the different social systems, states and regions.[39]

New thinking for Soviet foreign policy has been defined as thinking which is "consistently scientific and free from historically outdated stereotypes," and "reflects the realities of the contemporary world." By 1989, this definition was expanded to include elevation of the significance of "common human values" and morality in foreign policy, as well as the "de-ideologization of interstate relations."[40]

According to Gorbachev, awareness of the threat which nuclear war poses to the future of humanity, and the challenge of global problems which reflect the interdependence of all peoples require a shift by all countries away from the use of force to resolve differences. But most fundamentally, Gorbachev has identified ideology as part of the problem, because it is the central dynamic in the rivalry and hostility of the two camps. Thus the "de-ideologizing" of interstate relations is necessary if this hostility is to disappear.[41] In part, this call to remove ideology from interstate relations is directed at the West. Gorbachev has urged that all peoples "step over the things that divide us for the sake of the interests of all mankind, for the sake of life on Earth," and challenged the Western countries to rid their policy of "ideological prejudice" as the Soviets are doing.[42] Yet it is clear that Gorbachev also regards the Soviet Union's own ideological prejudices and Manichean world outlook as an obstacle to the kind of foreign policy that would best suit Soviet needs. He recently summarized the error of Soviet thinking as follows:

When we had just embarked upon restructuring, the party leadership was primarily concerned as to how matters were proceeding at home, within the country. But then, having begun to restructure, we very soon realized the need to rethink the entire situation worldwide, our own position in the world, our relations with the socialist countries and with states of a different social system; the totality of international relations and problems. In this way we arrived at the new political thinking and a rejection of outmoded notions and patterns, of the habit of seeing the world in black and white and we realized at least two important things. First, it is not possible to guarantee the security of one's own country without taking into account the security interests of other countries. . . . Second, in the modern interlinked and ever more integral world, progress is impossible in a society fenced off from the international process by sealed borders and ideological barriers.[43]

In a sense, Gorbachev is arguing that ideology is dysfunctional for Soviet foreign policy, that it gets in the way.

The indictment of ideology in foreign policy has several facets. At bottom, ideological differences and assumptions of mutual hostility could produce planetary devastation through nuclear war. Thus Deputy Foreign Minister Anatoli Adamishin has explained that ideology is dangerous and counterproductive in world politics because it is both coercive and offensive:

Why is injecting ideology into foreign policy so dangerous? The answer is that this is the direct path to foisting one's own views, scale of values and ideals. Hence intolerance of the opinions of others. Hence one step to the imposition of one's convictions by force. Few like this, as a rule. Therefore, the reaction is enmity, conflicts and war, which often boomerangs against the adherents of messianisms. Acts of ideological aggression do not remove ideological contradictions; they instigate tensions in international relations and create explosive situations. . . .

It is unacceptable for one side to assess the other as a freak of history, an ill-starred chance happening, a disease that must be cured, and to form its foreign policy on the basis of such an assessment. It is no less incorrect to suppose oneself the bearer of historical truth, the possessor of a patent on the future, and one's partners as temporary companions whose lives belong to the past and who have nothing to tell the generations to come.[44]

Gorbachev seems to recognize that the assumption that capitalist countries are implacable enemies is a self-fulfilling prophecy. Moreover, "zero-sum" thinking has promoted a search for military security against the capitalist world and hence to an expensive, cyclical arms race which has been an enormous burden on the Soviet economy, while military assistance for socialist and communist revolutionaries elsewhere has risked involvement in escalating East-West conflicts.

Gorbachev's proposal to discard ideology in interstate relations amounts to a judgment that the Cold War should be called off, and a pledge to accept peaceful coexistence with capitalist states as a more or less permanent condition. An ideological approach presumes an irreconcilable struggle, forecasts an eventual victory for socialism, and encourages combative rivalry. Thus a focus on ideological differences builds mistrust, suspicion, and reliance on coercive strategies rather than negotiated agreements. Gorbachev takes the position that a secular foreign policy can change Western perceptions of the USSR as an implacable enemy, weaken anti-Soviet political forces in Western governments and facilitate all sorts of mutually advantageous relationships that will reduce tension; but he must banish the USSR's own ideological thinking before he can pursue a secular policy. Thus the "de-ideologization" of foreign policy is a central premise of Gorbachev's reforms and a key to achievement of the kind of peaceful external environment which *perestroika* needs for success.

Ideological Revision as a Tool of Reform

Gorbachev's claim that ideology has no place in interstate relations is clearly provocative, and has required some careful justification. Predictably, Gorbachev has declared this approach to be truly Leninist, truly practical, and truly in conformity with contemporary realities.

A stress on the desirability of peaceful coexistence is hardly novel. However, Gorbachev has altered the established ways of talking about peaceful coexistence. Simply stressing the preferability of a world in which outstanding problems are solved without resort to force is not new. When the West or the U.S. is specifically blamed for causing all the conflicts and tension in the world, peaceful coexistence becomes just another propaganda slogan. Similarly, admonitions about the desirability of a "return to detente" can be just another way of criticizing the allegedly perfidious policies of the adversary.[45] But Gorbachev has developed his attack on "ideologized" foreign policy so as to buttress a new view of the West and a new view of Soviet interests which justify the kind of real compromises and concessions which can permit East-West arms control agreements, cuts in Soviet defense spending, and withdrawal from foreign conflict situations.

In his early comments on foreign affairs, Gorbachev followed a fairly "traditional" use of warnings about "the terrible threat to mankind" to argue that Soviet positions on arms control agreements were reasonable, and Western ones were not. Gorbachev proclaimed a Soviet preference for "stable, proper, and if you like, civilized inter-state relations."[46] He stressed that the danger of global war could be overcome "only if we learn to live together . . . by mastering the difficult art of respecting each other's interests. This we call the policy of peaceful coexistence."[47]

> We are ready to improve relations with the U.S. as well for mutual benefit and without attempts to impinge on the legitimate rights and interests of one another. There is no fatal inevitability of confrontation between the two countries.[48]

Gorbachev defended detente as an appropriate goal for East-West relations. Above all, he understood this to mean that all controversial issues and conflict situations "should be resolved by political means."[49]

Thus Gorbachev initially emphasized a conflict model of world politics in which Western policies are the major problem: "Through the fault of imperialism, the international situation remains tense and dangerous. . . . It must be stated in no uncertain terms that the responsibility for the present situation rests primarily with the ruling circles of the United States." The United States, he said, claims a "right to interfere everywhere," "constantly creates seats of conflict and military danger," continues to "sabotage disarmament," and plans through the Strategic Defense Initiative to militarize space. He concluded that international relations "could be channelled toward normal cooperation only if the imperialists abandon their attempts to solve the historical contest between the two systems by military means."[50]

Gorbachev reinforced this view that capitalist states are dangerous by emphasizing the need for countervailing power to control them. Thus he bragged about the "historic achievement" of military-strategic parity with NATO, a parity he said "must be protected by all means as a check on the appetites of imperialism." He also promised to "spare no efforts in providing the Soviet Armed Forces with everything necessary for defense."[51] As with previous pictures like this, however, it left the West capable of coming to its senses only through "political pressure" or the emergence of "sensible" leaders who could realize that militarist policies are futile and "adjust" their policies.

This analysis began to change in tandem with Gorbachev's increasingly radical domestic program. Instead of attacking the West, Gorbachev shifted to an attack on ideologically-based views of the world in which socialism and capitalism are in irreconcilable conflict. The draft program prepared for the 27th Party Congress (released in October, 1985) presented mixed messages. On the one hand, its characterization of imperialism (in crisis) and of the United States (responsible for the threat of war) were extremely hostile. Yet the Program also endorsed peaceful coexistence and said that spread of ideological contradictions between the two systems to interstate relations would be "inadmissible." Thus "the peoples' interests," according to the Program, demand interstate relations characterized by "peaceful competition and equal cooperation." As for Soviet-American relations, the Program called for "mutual understanding" and respect for "each other's legitimate interests."[52]

In his speech to the Party Congress, Gorbachev was more innovative. Citing "profound and significant" changes in the international environment, Gorbachev stated that the contemporary period was "perhaps the most alarming in history." He denied the Soviet Union was interested in "pushing revolution," and stressed that "no sensible solutions" to international problems could be found through force. Noting that the world has never been so "explosive," Gorbachev enjoined all states, without losing sight of "social, political, and ideological contradictions," to "master the science and the art of behaving with restraint and circumspection in the international arena." Gorbachev emphasized the global interdependence of all nations, and moved away from class categories by describing the party program as "profoundly humanist."[53]

By 1987, Gorbachev's plea for the "de-ideologization" of international politics had become bolder and more direct. His book *Perestroika: New Thinking for Our Country and the World*, which was widely distributed in the West, linked this need to banish ideology to the nuclear threat:

> Ideological differences should not be transferred to the sphere of interstate relations, nor should foreign policy be subordinate to them, for ideologies may be poles apart, whereas the interest of survival and prevention of war stand universal and supreme.[54]

Qualifications and clarifications have been added. Thus Gorbachev has stressed that "we are not giving up our convictions, philosophy, or traditions," or refusing to recognize "the real state of affairs, the existence of social systems based on different forms of property and different ideologies." Nonetheless, he has affirmed that the "honest struggle of ideology" should not spill over into interstate relations.[55]

A new view of world trends has emerged to complement this view that ideology is dangerous in interstate relations. This new world view helps to explain why "concern for the common fate of humanity" now takes precedence over class interests, but seems to depart rather substantially from accepted Leninist interpretations of historical developments. Under previous Soviet leaders, party documents had regularly

Ideology and Foreign Policy

described the world arena as full of conflict, and had provided assessments of the state of the "balance of forces" in the struggle between forces of progress and forces of reaction. Indeed, in 1983 Gorbachev himself had made such a statement:

> The time we live in will go down in history as a time of intense class struggle in the world arena. There are sharp clashes between two lines, two diametrically opposed approaches to international relations."[56]

But by the Party Congress in 1986, Gorbachev had a different view. Instead, he put forward a description of a world so threatened by destructive disasters that such struggle was impermissible:

> We are realists and are perfectly well aware that the two worlds are divided by very many things, and deeply divided too. But we also see clearly that the need to resolve most vital problems affecting all humanity must prompt them to interaction, awakening humanity's heretofore unseen powers of self-preservation. . . . The course of history, of social progress, requires ever more insistently that there should be constructive and creative interaction between states and peoples on the scale of the entire world. . . . Such interaction is essential in order to prevent nuclear catastrophe, in order that civilization could survive. It is essential in order that other worldwide problems that are growing more acute should also be resolved jointly in the interests of all concerned. The realistic dialectics of present-day development consist in a combination of competition and confrontation between the two systems and in a growing tendency towards interdependence of the countries of the world community. This is precisely the way, through the struggle of opposites, through arduous effort, groping in the dark to some extent, as it were, that the contradictory but interdependent and in many ways integral world is taking shape. . . .
>
> We proceed from the premise that the main direction of struggle in contemporary conditions is to create worthy, truly human material and spiritual conditions of life for all nations, to see to it that our planet should be habitable, and to deal with its riches rationally.[57]

Thus Gorbachev concluded that the "dialectics" of the world mean that violent struggle between progressive and regressive societies cannot occur, since the possibility of nuclear devastation had set an "objective limit" to class struggle between nations. Competition between capitalist and socialist states is inevitable, he has said, but "it must be kept within a framework of peaceful competition which necessarily envisages cooperation." This competition should not be to see which system can defeat the other, but to demonstrate which system has the greater capacity to meet human needs.[58]

As he has developed his ideas about appropriate East-West relations, Gorbachev has taken up the theme of national interest. This is a way of emphasizing that the USSR has interests which are "normal" and deserve respect (such as the need for good relations with its neighbor, Afghanistan), and have little to do with ideology. All other states have such interests too, which means that these normal and respectable interests can form the basis for agreements between states with very different ideologies.[59] Recently Gorbachev reaffirmed this view:

> We see our responsibility, of course, we are defending our interests, but we are prepared to take account of the views of others, and we also presuppose the responsibility of other countries for changing the situation in the world for the better, and for moving on to the new thinking.[60]

Justification for such a non-ideological, accommodating approach is found in the early diplomacy of the young Soviet state: the Brest-Litovsk peace treaty with the Germans, participation in the Genoa conference of 1922, and a series of treaties with non-socialist bordering states (Iran, Turkey and Afghanistan). References to "legitimate interests of both sides" were also characteristic language of Soviet-American statements during the detente period.

Some Soviets have gone beyond Gorbachev, insisting that the common danger of nuclear war is a poor argument for setting aside ideology in interstate relations, since that would suggest that once the danger of nuclear war were past, ideological struggle and conflict would return.[61] Something much more permanent is intended:

> We still need to analyze and ponder a great deal, assessing the prospects for international relations in the light of the new thinking. But it is already quite clear that cohabitation between the two systems is not a mere breathing space, as many people thought in the twenties, and not a special form of class struggle, as we believed not so long ago, but a form of mutually beneficial interstate cooperation given, of course, the existence of ideological differences and class contradictions.
>
> On the other hand, cooperation by no means implies that one system should be equated with and attuned to another, or, for instance, that there should be any convergence.[62]

The question of the ultimate path of such "quiet rivalry" between the two social systems is intriguing. One commentator has suggested that the rivalry will "continue in forms that don't end, it will continue in forms that don't spell catastrophe for mankind so that in the future there can be a synthesis of both policies and a peaceful, evolutionary emergence of universal forms of social life, suitable for future generations." Others are more careful to deny that any "blending" is anticipated.[63]

Gorbachev has said that recognizing the priority for human values is the "backbone" of the new political thinking[64] and has professed a willingness to bring down many of the barriers between socialists and capitalists. His descriptions of Soviet foreign policy so downplay confrontation and struggle that they may well raise questions about how far capitalist-socialist cooperation should go:

> Our foreign policy, which is based on the principle of freedom of choice, de-ideologizing of interstate relations, balance of interests, and internationalization of many problems, is open to contacts and cooperation with the most varied forces of the present world. As it turns out, we are able to find a common language and the necessary modicum of mutual understanding with the representatives of such circles and such states with which, as it seemed, we could quite recently have nothing in common.[65]

Banishing a confrontational approach to international relations is what downgrading "class interests" means. This makes many things possible and appropriate: openness to foreign visitors and foreign information, participation in international economic and financial institutions, and friendly relations with states of all kinds. Acceptance of the Soviet Union's own responsibility for East-West hostility justifies efforts to build trust in Soviet good faith through negotiating concessions, settlements of regional conflicts and unilateral confidence-building gestures. The theoretical and practical implications of this new world view are the subject of the following sections.

Banishing the Class Struggle

The role of ideology in Soviet foreign policy has certainly declined; however, justifying a secular foreign policy is itself an ideological problem. Gorbachev advocates three themes which are particularly controversial: the subordination of class interests to human interests, the rejection of peaceful coexistence as a form of class struggle, and a revised appraisal of capitalist society and the prospects for socialist revolutions there.

According to Gorbachev, the fact that the party's new program deliberately removed a reference to peaceful coexistence "as a specific form of class struggle" does not mean the Soviets have given up class analysis. Thus while noting that "a class-motivated approach" is the "ABC of Marxism" and still appropriate inside "class-divided countries," he argues that the possibility of global destruction has introduced "an objective limit for class confrontation in the international arena." Gorbachev also claims that the priority for "interests common to all humanity over class interests" is ideologically correct, since Lenin spoke "more than once" about "the priority of interests common to all humanity over class interests."[66] Soviet scholars back up this argument by citing a work of 1897 in which Lenin said that "the interests of societal development stand above the interests of the proletariat," just as the interests of the workers movement as a whole take precedence over the interests of one of its elements.[67]

There may well have been some resistance to Gorbachev's formulations. While Gorbachev again cited "Lenin's idea of the priority of the interests of social development" in his 70th revolutionary anniversary speech in November 1987, he actually gave the nod to class forces with a statement that "the class struggle and other manifestations of social contradictions will exert influence on the objective processes in favor of peace."[68] However, in a speech to a meeting of representatives of parties and movements who attended the anniversary celebrations, Gorbachev not only insisted that one could no longer study world development "merely from the viewpoint of a struggle between two opposing social systems," but asserted that the class interests of socialism "as a system" and "general human interests" are fused.[69] By the time of the February, 1988 Central Committee plenum on ideology, Gorbachev was back on the offensive. He declared once again that the USSR's new political thinking included "a sincere rejection of the ideologization of international relations," and restated his idea that "general human values" were central to the new thinking:

> The fundamental theoretical question currently facing both Marxists and their opponents is the question of combining class-based and general human principles in real world development and consequently in politics.[70]

Gorbachev's speech to the June 1988, Party conference suggested that although international relations were not losing their class nature, they were "being increasingly realized as relations among people." He depicted a future in which international relations would be "gradually demilitarized and humanized."[71]

In December 1988, Gorbachev proclaimed to the United Nations General Assembly that "the de-ideologization of interstate relations has become a demand of the new age." Together, he said, all peoples must pursue "supremacy of the common human idea." The framework for this discussion of ideology was a plea for tolerance, and "respect for other people's views and stands." Gorbachev insisted "we are not giving up our convictions, philosophy, or traditions" nor asking anyone else to do so.[72] More recently he has defended his view vigorously, and has rejected "absurd accusations" that he was yielding positions, abandoning class approaches and the interests of the national liberation movement:

> As is well known, the new political thinking presupposes taking the ideology out of interstate relations. But that certainly does not mean, as some people want to interpret it, taking the ideology out of international relations. No, that would be a refusal to recognize the real state of affairs, the existence of social systems based on different forms of property and on different ideologies. We can see the depth of the differences between the two social systems, but that is not a reason for opposition by force and the confrontation of states.

However, Gorbachev did admit that "we have fallen behind in the elaboration of the dialectics of the correlation of values common to all mankind and class interests, and our science has something to work on here."[73]

Several writers have pointed out that "ideologization" of international relations suits socialism's enemies, and is an old tactic of rabid anticommunists.[74] This is a not-so-subtle way of suggesting that what Gorbachev's critics want may aid the enemy—or at least would make things worse.

Peaceful Coexistence and the Priority of Human Values

In the Marxist-Leninist world view, the struggle between socialism and capitalism has been the central dynamic. Gorbachev's proposal to remove ideology from interstate relations suggests that the threat of nuclear destruction has indefinitely postponed this struggle. Gorbachev has recalled that this struggle was temporarily set aside once before, during the wartime coalition against Hitler—an event, he says that showed that "common interests" can be put ahead of sociopolitical ones.[75]

What about peaceful coexistence? As a position that justifies some level of political accommodation with "class enemies" peaceful coexistence is a well-established concept. Nikita Khrushchev made a shift to a of peaceful coexistence a major emphasis of his foreign policy. However, as put forward in the Party Program of 1961, this peaceful coexistence was linked to a thoroughly hostile view of capitalist states. According to that analysis, what made peaceful coexistence possible was the combined strength of socialist states and their associates and allies; what made peaceful coexistence necessary was the lethal quality of thermonuclear war. Moreover, it was defined as a policy which was mindful of the differences between socioeconomic systems:

> Peaceful coexistence serves as a basis for the peaceful competition between socialism and capitalism on an international scale and constitutes a specific form of class struggle between them. As they consistently pursue the policy of peaceful coexistence, the socialist countries are steadily strengthening the positions of the world socialist system in its competition with capitalism. Peaceful coexistence affords more favorable opportunities for the struggle of the working class in the capitalist countries and facilitates the struggle of the peoples of the colonial and dependent countries for their liberation. Support for the principle of peaceful coexistence is also in keeping with the interests of that section of the bourgeoisie which realizes that a thermonuclear war would not spare the ruling classes of capitalist society either. The policy of peaceful coexistence is in accord with the vital interests of all mankind, except the big monopoly magnates and the militarists.

To be sure, the 1961 Program presented a somewhat contradictory analysis, in which war was undesirable, but would be useful if it occurred:

> Peaceful coexistence of the socialist and capitalist countries is an objective necessity for the development of human society. War cannot and must not serve as a means of settling international disputes. Peaceful coexistence or disastrous war—such is the alternative offered by history. Should the imperialist aggressors nevertheless venture to start a new world war, the peoples will no longer tolerate a system which drags them into devastating wars. They will sweep imperialism away and bury it. Peaceful coexistence implies renunciation of war as a means of settling international disputes, and their solution by negotiation. . . .[76]

Gorbachev has made it clear that the new Draft Party Program of 1986 chose very deliberately to reject this formulation as inappropriate, because admitting the possibility of nuclear war would be "unrealistic." Today, he has emphasized, peaceful coexistence is not a form of class struggle, for social progress depends on preventing war.[77]

Vadim Medvedev has explained that Lenin came to see peaceful coexistence as a "fundamental law of the age" once he had concluded that revolutionary pressure could not resolve the historical conflict between capitalism and socialism. However, this principle had later been "deformed." Thus peaceful coexistence came to mean simply postponing the "virtually inevitable" war with capitalism, while the two-camp view of the Cold War period "reinforced confrontational trends." Even for Khrushchev, peaceful coexistence was not expected to last. Medvedev argues that the current Soviet leadership regards world coexistence as "a long-term ongoing process with historical boundaries that are difficult to define."[78] Others have criticized the ambiguity of the earlier formulation of peaceful coexistence as a form of class struggle, and imply it should not be taken seriously since it emerged "in the heat of polemics with the Maoists."[79]

The new priority for human values is closely related to these ideas. On many occasions, Gorbachev has simply equated "human values" with human survival. In other words, putting human values ahead of class interests is another way of saying that avoiding nuclear war is the top Soviet foreign policy goal. Thus promoting progressive political changes and socialist revolutions, or competing for supremacy or "victory" over capitalist societies are not appropriate if these activities involve a risk of nuclear war.

It should also be noted that an analysis which identifies class interests as relatively less important than universal human values provides opportunities to emphasize what is shared across cultures and socioeconomic systems. This has served very conveniently to justify Gorbachev's domestic political reforms, by supporting the idea of copying or borrowing democratic forms and norms from Western societies. Vadim Medvedev has said that since socialism continues the best traditions of democracy and humanism, "it would be inadmissibly sectarian and politically limited to refuse to make critical and creative use of those democratic forms which are the result of social progress and are essentially the property of common human cultures." Socialism must "inherit the best of everything produced by previous historical development."[80]

Putting universal human values first also helps to promote and justify Gorbachev's preference for a Soviet Union that is more open to the West, and to Western ideas and practices. This emphasis has also promoted claims that socialism as a value system shares a great deal with other value systems, and can, for example, agree that the Ten Commandments are an appropriate standard for human behavior:

> People's attention is focused on their differences to such an extent that the values that link them are often overshadowed. However, universal values are not an invented category. It includes quite real notions, namely, life, the continuation of the human race, the environment, world culture, scientific and technological advance, and the health of the individual and of humanity. Common values include the family, the dignity of the individual, mutual assistance and solidarity, and much else.
>
> In addition to everything else, these are the most solid values. In the final analysis, it is simply profitable to be guided by the ten commandments. Common sense reaffirms this at each step of everyday life. It has to be made the guiding force in international affairs.[81]

Thus Gorbachev's approach to the role of ideology in foreign policy can imply an extremely eclectic approach which emphasizes not the distinctiveness of Soviet culture, but the elements it shares with others. Apparently there is some concern that value distinctions are being devalued. At least, some Soviet scholars have sought to clarify how coexistence in the service of human values can go forward without blurring essential value differences or promoting "convergence" of beliefs.[82]

New Views of the Class Enemy

Taking ideology out of interstate relations and putting human interests ahead of class interests are closely related to a new view of the

West, particularly the sources of its foreign policy and the prospects for its social development. Here too, Gorbachev's views have evolved over time. At first he depicted Western societies in traditional terms as in social decline, and therefore especially dangerous internationally. As he grew more eager for Soviet-American rapprochement, he emphasized the possibility that Western leaders could be persuaded of the value of more rational and less belligerent policies. As he said in November, 1987:

> We are by no means seeking to get our class adversary to "fall in love" with us. We do not need that at all. What we are counting on is the fact that life will compel him to take realities into account and to become aware that we are all in the same boat and that we must behave in such a way that it does not capsize.

But where traditional analyses point out that militarism is part of capitalist society, Gorbachev chose to stress that aggressive Western behavior is a matter of *choice:*

> You may have noted that . . . I spoke of two particularly dangerous manifestations of capitalist laws: militarization and the unequal exchange with the developing world. However, these are only possible with the aid of appropriate state policy—and this policy enjoys support; it enjoys support for as long as the fear of the Soviet military threat persists; for as long as people are firmly convinced that there exist superior national interests and that there exist those of secondary importance; that there are subjects of world politics and economics and that there are objects, that is, the neocolonialist sphere.
>
> With all its international consequences, our restructuring is demolishing the fear of the Soviet military threat and militarism loses its political justification.[83]

This approach drops the idea that the West is necessarily inherently hostile to the USSR. Instead, Western hostility is understood conditionally, as a policy determined by a variety of external and internal forces. This permits Gorbachev to examine the ways in which Soviet behavior affects Western attitudes through its impact on leaders and on public opinion, and to undertake initiatives designed to encourage these governments to change their policies. One Soviet academic recently supported this analysis by asking why Soviets should assume that capitalists cannot be reasonable, citing Reagan's gradual abandonment of extreme hostility to the USSR as proof of the benefits of "de-ideologizing" interstate relations.[84]

Gorbachev and others have made it clear that peaceful coexistence is an imperative for inter*state* relations, whereas class struggle is a concept relevant only within states. These clarifications have not done much to encourage revolutionary optimism, since Gorbachev has also made it clear that the priority for human over class interests applies to communists everywhere. Advice to foreign communists has been to take account of the "new realities" and, among other things, avoid armed revolutionary struggle:

> The struggle of opposing class forces does not disappear in the nuclear age. But our times teach us to develop and make widespread use of compromise forms of struggle as well. There is no departure from revolutionary Marxism whatsoever in such actions.[85]

Meanwhile, analyses of Western society have helped to justify downgrading class interests by discounting the prospects for socialist revolutions there. One aspect of the new "realism" about capitalist societies emphasizes that socialism is simply not an attractive alternative:

> Capitalism's ability to adapt to the new historical environment has exceeded our expectations. The prospect of socialist transformations in developed capitalist countries has been put off to the indefinite future. . . . Socialism has not yet been able to acquire the force of example of which Lenin spoke.[86]

Several scholars have now explained that Lenin and Marx were simply wrong. While they assumed that capitalism had exhausted its potential, capitalism has found new vitality. While they assumed that communist revolutions were imminent, "this is not what happened."[87] Analyses of contemporary capitalist society have emphasized that "class" thinking is not popular, the masses are not revolutionary, and the social structure doesn't coincide with the "working class-bourgeoisie" antagonism.[88] One Soviet commentator has been quoted as saying bluntly that "world revolution is not on the agenda."[89] Of course Gorbachev has denied he means to change the view that imperialism is a bad sociopolitical system, but current Soviet descriptions of the vitality of Western society are in vivid contrast with previously ubiquitous claims that capitalism was an abhorrent system in deep crisis.

Orthodox Challenges

Not everyone in the Soviet Union is happy with the "new thinking," enthusiastic about the calls for radical reform, or comfortable with the changes in policies and institutions which are occurring. Gorbachev regularly complains about "inertia" and resistance of conservative forces threatened by the reforms. While increasingly careful to present himself as a centrist, balancing dangers from conservatives against the dangers from the "overzealous and impatient," Gorbachev clearly seems most concerned about those who resist the reforms on ideological or practical grounds, who say the reforms "erode principles," or who "sow the seeds of doubt."[90] He has complained that "some are nostalgic for the good old days" and believe that the country needs "a firm hand," but has repeatedly charged that his critics are selfishly motivated—or as he put it recently, have been "torn away from their feeding troughs."[91]

Gorbachev acknowledges that *perestroika* is a "complex and contradictory process," a "revolutionary" and "difficult" time. He admits that much has occurred to irritate people, and has been frank about shortages which encourage continued controversy over the merits and motives of reform:

> Restructuring has literally blown up the illusory peace and harmony which reigned supreme in this country in the years of torpor, kicked off broad-based and free-wheeling debates and put the spotlight on many urgent and even painful issues.

Nonetheless Gorbachev calls upon Soviet citizens "not to lose heart" or "panic" in spite of the tasks ahead and the controversies about how to solve them, and has done his best to reassure those who might be "confused."[92]

The only coherent statement of opposition to the ideological aspects of Gorbachev's reforms to appear to date is a long letter to the editors of *Sovetskaia Rossiya* by a teacher named Nina Andreyeva. This letter, which was printed in March 1988, appears to have been intended as a response not only to Gorbachev's February 1988 speech on ideology, but to the larger assault on the historical and ideological justifications of existing institutions and practices. Ms. Andreyeva took a strong stand against any compromise of principles, hinting that *perestroika* and *glasnost'* were promoting intellectual and ideological anarchy. Her letter takes on added significance in the light of apparent links to Yegor Ligachev, a Politburo member who has publicly criticized some aspects of Gorbachev's reforms.[93]

Andreyeva expressed dismay at the negative side effects of *perestroika,* and complained about "nihilism," "ideological confusion" and "disorientation" produced by the reformers' attacks on Soviet history, on past leaders (including Stalin) and on Soviet society. The letter derided efforts to be "businesslike and pragmatic" or to "kowtow" to the "real and supposed achievements of Western capitalist societies." She attacked the individualism of humanist "left wing liberal intellectual socialism" and challenged the idea that "the class struggle is obsolete" in interstate relations.

Although it was more than three weeks before an official rejoinder appeared, the response from Gorbachev and his associates was both harsh and comprehensive. *Pravda*'s rebuttal accused Ms. Andreyeva of "providing an ideological platform and manifesto for anti-restructuring forces" from an "essentially conservative and dogmatic" position. Again acknowledging "confusion" about the reforms and their implications for accepted ideological principles, the editorial hotly defended the necessity for *perestroika* and a decisive break with methods of the past:

> Do we have the right, in the face of the real difficulties and unsatisfied needs of the people, to adhere to the same old approaches which prevailed in the thirties and forties? Has not the time come to clearly differentiate between the essence of socialism and the historically restricted forms of its implementation? Has not the time come for a scientifically critical investigation of our history, primarily in order to change the world in which we are living and to learn harsh lessons for the future?[94]

Citing an urgent need for unity, the editorial castigated Andreyeva's letter for inciting disaffection and hinted that her views were selfishly motivated:

> It is an axiom of Marxism that ideas and interests are mutually linked categories. Any interest is expressed in certain ideas. Behind all ideas there is invariably a particular interest. Conservative opposition to restructuring is composed of the weight of custom and habitual thinking and action derived from the past and the belligerent, selfish interests of those accustomed to living at others' expense and reluctant to kick this habit. It is against those interests that restructuring is objectively aimed, for restructuring, like every revolution, is not just for something, it is also against something. It is against everything that impedes our living a better, cleaner, and fuller life, making more rapid progress and paying the least price for the inevitable mistakes and miscalculations that occur along the new path.

The editorial also suggested that Andreyeva's position was close to treason by pointing out that the "positions of home-grown mourners of socialism coincide with the positions of socialism's opponents abroad." Perhaps more to the point, *Pravda* rebuked Andreyeva for attacking party policy.

A rebuttal of Andreyeva's letter published in a prominent foreign affairs journal essentially accused her of looking for enemies, just the kind of paranoia which justified Stalin's authoritarianism and had prevented the Soviet government from seeking ways to reduce international tension in the past. Moreover, her views were criticized for promoting an understanding of the USSR as the "organ" of the international working class—a view which would provide an excuse for Soviet expansionism.[95]

Although no more "platforms" have appeared, Yegor Ligachev (shifted from ideology to agriculture in October, 1988) did publicly challenge Gorbachev's ideas about the reduced importance of class interests internationally. In August, 1988, Ligachev set himself against the priority for "universal human values" by stating that "we proceed from the class character of international relations." "Raising the question in another way," he said, "only confuses the minds of the Soviet people and our friends abroad." Thus he insisted that the new approach did not mean "artificial 'deceleration' of social and national liberation struggle."[96] Aleksander Yakovlev (a Gorbachev supporter recently elevated to the Politburo and to the head of the new Central Committee Commission on International Affairs) quickly responded with a defense of the importance of common human interests and affirmed that the "founders of socialism" certainly never meant to set class interests against all other interests:

> Marxism as such is the interpretation of common human interests from the viewpoint of the history and future development of all mankind, not only individual countries or classes, peoples or social groups.[97]

For the present it is quite obvious that Gorbachev rules the "commanding heights" of ideology, and it is difficult to judge the extent of dissent. Gorbachev has sought to confine debates about the reforms to administrative and practical matters by insisting that the need for *perestroika* is incontrovertible and objective. Thus those who resist the reforms are depicted as defenders of ineffective policies, or as stubborn, selfish conservatives who lack community spirit. While acknowledging that Soviet citizens have legitimate reasons to complain about shortages, Gorbachev has blamed these "market imbalances" on mismanagement and poor labor discipline, but also on "lack of understanding" and "direct opposition" to some of the new policies.[98] While he appears to have confidence that the practical results of improved economic mechanisms and more effective social policy will reconcile the doubters, Gorbachev is clearly intolerant of any systematic ideological critiques which might challenge the ideological orthodoxy of his reforms. Conservative hostility to the call for ideological creativity is not the only problem, however. The policy of *glasnost'* and the encouragement given to citizen involvement in government have produced a wide spectrum of controversy and challenges, including many who want the reforms to go further. At a time of rapid change, discontent has many roots.

Foreign Policy Self-Criticism

The "new political thinking" has built on some severe and unusual criticisms of the USSR's foreign policy. Gorbachev has charged that past Soviet leaders were preoccupied with East-West conflict to the detriment both of Soviet national interests and of world peace. He has also identified a number of faults in the working style of Soviet diplomats and in the foreign policy decision-making process that require correction. The intellectual foundations of foreign policy analysis need work: Gorbachev has called upon his experts to test their ideas against reality, and rethink established interpretations of world developments.

Errors of the Past

The most striking aspect of Soviet discussions of foreign policy under Gorbachev is their emphasis on Soviet responsibility for the state of East-West relations. In his book, *Perestroika*, Gorbachev charged that some of the errors of Soviet foreign policy resulted from "improvident reaction to American actions."[99] Without being too specific, Gorbachev has cited past "mistakes:"

> It was not always and not everywhere, before and after World War II, that we succeeded in making use of the opportunities opening up. We were unable to make use of the enormous moral prestige with which the Soviet Union emerged from the war to consolidate the peace-loving, democratic forces and stop the organizers of the cold war.[100]

In May 1988, the Central Committee published Theses for the Extraordinary 19th Party Congress scheduled for June. The tenth thesis, which deals with foreign policy, brought together and articulated key elements of Gorbachev's approach. Errors of the past were an important theme: "A critical analysis of the past has shown that dogmatism and the subjectivist approach has also left a mark on our foreign policy." Opportunities for reducing tension were missed, and the USSR "allowed itself to be drawn into the arms race."[101]

In his speech to the Party Conference itself, Gorbachev expanded his complaints about "command-administrative methods" into both a conceptual and managerial critique of his predecessors' foreign policy:

> It even happened that decisions of major importance were made by a narrow circle of persons, without a collective, all-round examination and analysis, and sometimes without due consultation with our friends. This led to an inadequate reaction to international events and to the policies of other states, and even to erroneous decisions. Unfortunately, it was not always weighed up what one or another option for action would cost the people or what it could result in. In response to the nuclear challenge thrown down to us and to the whole socialist world, it was essential to achieve strategic parity with the United States. That was done. However, having concentrated vast resources and attention on the military aspect of opposition to imperialism, we did not always use the political opportunities offered by fundamental changes in the world to ensure the state's security and to reduce tension and achieve mutual understanding among the peoples. As a result, we allowed ourselves to be drawn into the arms race, which could not fail to have an effect on the country's socioeconomic development and on its international position. The arms race, moreover, was coming close to the critical point.[102]

Publication of the Theses prompted considerable discussion of the quality of foreign policy decision-making, and provided a stimulus to those eager to endorse Gorbachev's new approaches by criticizing the past, and to call for more *glasnost'*—more discussion and debate about foreign policy. Soviet responsibility for East-West tension was an important theme in these discussions.

Foreign Minister Shevardnadze took up the criticism of specific foreign policies, citing the deployment of SS-20s, the invasion of Afghanistan and the buildup of chemical weapons as examples of recent foreign policy errors.[103] A deputy department director within the Ministry of Foreign Affairs has embellished this critique by attacking "ideologists of attrition" among the bureaucrats who damaged Soviet interests by recommending poorly thought out and unrealistic foreign policy goals.[104] One commentator asked "Who stood up and said that [deployment of SS-20s] was an invitation to bring the Pershings into Western Europe?"[105] And despite the delicacy with which the top leadership has handled the Afghanistan invasion, academician V. I. Dashichev was not afraid to denounce it:

> It seems to me that, when the decision was made to send our troops into Afghanistan (even though that was done at the Afghan government's request), all the possible consequences of this step were not thoroughly

> weighed. .... It is perfectly clear that this step contributed to a most serious aggravation of relations between the Soviet Union and the United States and the other Western powers, it had a most negative effect on the easing of international tension, and in my opinion, it gave a powerful boost to the arms race.[106]

Admissions of error clearly help to justify changes in foreign policy and in its ideological underpinnings and major assumptions.

If Soviet foreign policy errors have contributed to East-West tension, this raises the question who is threatening whom.

> Is it not time to ask ourselves whether or not the principles of Soviet military development and our foreign policy conduct in the past years had something that gave "the other side" at least a cause for concern?[107]

Dashichev has said that the Soviet Union itself has been guilty of "hegemonism" in its foreign policy, and bears responsibility for the shape of World War II. In his view, labelling the West as aggressive for resisting Soviet advances ignores all the things the USSR has done to arouse fears:

> In the eyes of the overwhelming proportion of the Western public the Soviet Union is a dangerous power whose leadership wants to eliminate the bourgeois democracies by military means and to establish a Soviet-type communist system throughout the world.

Dashichev has also blamed Brezhnev's Third World expansionism for the failure of detente. By contrast, he praises Soviet leaders of the past who overcame "dangerous illusions about 'world revolution.' "[108]

Has the Western threat been overestimated? In remarks to foreign journalists, Oleg Bogomolov, Dashichev's boss at the Institute of Economics of the World Socialist System, seemed to say so:

> The Theses now note that we do not discount the militarist danger contained in the nature of imperialism. Of course, we know many examples of major Western powers demonstrating aggressiveness with regard to small countries; we can see the military pressure in the Persian Gulf, and so forth. Nonetheless, the thesis of the unvarying nature of imperialism is somehow not very dialectic. Because everything develops, and in particular, the situation in Europe today is absolutely different from what it was on the eve of World War II. The Western countries' economic base is also changing. Today the process of interweaving, of interdependence, has, thanks to the activity of the multinational corporations, acquired utterly different dimensions and gone so far that any major

military clash becomes increasingly less likely. So even on the theoretical plane, the question of the threat and the degree of threat must be compared with the realities.[109]

Gorbachev has been especially forceful about the need to change the USSR's image, and to banish the idea that the Soviet Union is a threat to the West. On several occasions Gorbachev has referred to Khrushchev's famous outburst, "We will bury you!" as responsible even today for anti-Soviet hysteria. He also has said that East-West relations won't improve if one side is "mesmerized by ideological myths."[110] Foreign Minister Shevardnadze has echoed this point, criticizing errors of the past which built up the "'enemy image' on whose demolition we are now expending so much effort."[111]

Improving the Quality of Foreign Policy Decision-making

Gorbachev has criticized "stereotypes and cliches," "dogmatism," "inertia," "prejudice, complacency and stagnation" within the diplomatic service, and denounced "senseless stubbornness" in negotiations. In contrast, he has praised realistic approaches which would increase the possibility of agreements and mutually beneficial dealings with other states:

> When planning foreign policy, it is necessary to make a more sober and broader evaluation of the specific facts, rather than viewing everything only from the point of view of one's own interests. Because if every country pursues only its own interests and is incapable of meeting its partner halfway, of seeking points of contact, and of cooperating with that partner, then it will be difficult to achieve any improvement in international relations.[112]

Willingness to make concessions for the sake of a balance of interests, and to establish "normal, businesslike relations" with capitalist countries are in the national interest, Gorbachev has said, because they will undermine anti-Soviet attitudes.[113]

Secrecy and isolation have also been criticized. Gorbachev has stressed the value of "direct communication" with both governments and peoples of other states which "opens the Soviet Union anew to the outside world" and helps to break down stereotypes which play into the hands of socialism's enemies. Contact with the outside world also provides useful "feedback" which Gorbachev claims enhances the acceptability of Soviet proposals.[114] Accordingly, Gorbachev has urged that foreign policy making be "democratized," and the 19th Party Conference recommended that the Supreme Soviet should play a central role in the formulation of foreign policy. Foreign Minister Shevardnadze has endorsed the idea that legislative commissions of the Supreme Soviet should hold hearings to review policy options, and have overall control over the military budget and any use of military forces outside the USSR.[115] Citing "foreign policy elitism" as one source of "blunders, omissions and incompetence," Dashichev has high praise for Shevardnadze's commitment to widening the process, and involving specialists as well as the general public.[116] Gorbachev's determination to widen the decision-making process was affirmed at the Congress of People's Deputies in June, 1989—although the resolution demanding "people's control" of foreign policy in order to rule out "undemocratic" decisions may produce new dilemmas.

Cost-effectiveness is another theme endorsed by Gorbachev, another way to show how preoccupation with countering imperialism impeded more sensible policies which could better serve Soviet interests. Shevardnadze has complained about "vast material investment in hopeless foreign policy projects" which "are costing our people a lot to this day," and has regularly stressed that foreign policy should be in harmony with resources and capabilities.[117]

Ideological Revision and Gorbachev's Foreign Policy Goals

Gorbachev's redefined view of world politics supports a number of innovative policies. His determination to reduce East-West hostility has brought major initiatives in arms control and national security policy, and in the settlement of regional conflicts. The USSR has distanced itself somewhat from Third World radical regimes, taken steps to improve relations with a broad variety of states, and moved to enlarge its participation in multilateral political and financial institutions.

Security Policy

Gorbachev's arms control initiatives have provided the most dramatic illustrations of his determination to dispel hostile Western images of the USSR. Arms control negotiations had been broken off by the Soviets at the end of 1983. While American and Soviet negotiating positions on strategic arms reductions were far apart, the major issues were NATO deployments of intermediate nuclear weapons (justified as a response to extensive Soviet deployments of SS-20 intermediate range missiles), and the announcement of U.S. plans for a strategic defense initiative (SDI). A foreign ministers meeting in January 1985 had agreed that parallel talks would resume on all three types of weapons: long and intermediate range offensive systems, and defensive and space-based weapons.

Gorbachev became an active campaigner for arms control agreements within this framework, and introduced a series of proposals that included some important concessions to Western positions. In August 1985, he announced a unilateral moratorium on nuclear weapons tests, and proposed a moratorium on INF deployment. A Reagan-Gorbachev summit at Geneva in November 1985 produced a statement confirming that both sides believed a nuclear war "could not be won and should never be fought," and a pledge to prevent an arms race in space, reduce nuclear weapons by 50 percent, and enhance strategic stability. Nonetheless serious differences existed over how to accomplish these goals. The

Soviets sought to link arms reductions to reaffirmations of the ABM treaty constraints on defensive systems, while the United States was committed to a transition to defensive deterrence.

In January 1986, Gorbachev proposed that reductions in strategic weapons proceed in stages so that all nuclear weapons would be eliminated by the year 2000, and indicated a willingness to consider signing an agreement on intermediate range weapons separately. Although the U.S. announced in May 1986 that it would no longer be bound by the limits of the SALT II treaty of 1979 (which, although unratified, had been observed by both sides), and in June declared its view that the ABM treaty could be interpreted to permit work on the strategic defense initiative, Soviet efforts to move the negotiations along continued. At a Reagan-Gorbachev summit at Reykjavik, Iceland in November 1986, Gorbachev countered a U.S. proposal to eliminate all ICBM's with one to eliminate all nuclear weapons provided SDI were stopped. While Reagan rejected this package, the two leaders did agree on the desirability of an accord which would commit both powers to the ABM treaty for an agreed period. The summit produced agreement on specific limits of 1600 strategic delivery vehicles and 6,000 warheads which would guide subsequent strategic arms talks. In 1987, Gorbachev cleared the way for a separate INF treaty by accepting on-site verification and a complete elimination of both U.S. and Soviet intermediate range nuclear weapons. The INF treaty was signed in December, 1987 at a Soviet-American summit which also issued an ambiguous statement about the ways in which affirmation of the ABM treaty would be linked with an agreement on strategic arms reduction. These developments have facilitated significant progress on specific proposals for reductions and limitations on strategic arms. A joint draft treaty text has been prepared, but important disagreements remain and have so far not permitted final agreement.

Meanwhile, Gorbachev's aggressive approach to arms control matters has also reinvigorated conventional arms negotiations. A multilateral agreement on confidence building measures in Europe was reached in 1986 and signed at Stockholm in December. In 1988, the twenty-three members of NATO and the Warsaw Treaty Organization agreed to a new forum for conventional force reduction negotiations known as the Negotiations on Conventional Forces in Europe (CFE). These took on new interest in December 1988 when Gorbachev announced potentially significant unilateral cuts in manpower and equipment, and put forward goals for asymmetrical reductions to equal force levels which were below those in the initial NATO proposals.[118]

Gorbachev has defended these "concessions" as productive expressions of the "new thinking"—proof of Soviet readiness for "compromise on an equal basis, without detriment to anyone's security." He points to the INF treaty and the improvement in East-West relations as a major achievement of his administration, and claims credit for helping to make the world a safer place.[119]

The risk of nuclear war, and the possible annihilation of mankind, are at the heart of the "new realities" Gorbachev has said must guide Soviet policy. It is not new to argue that the potential devastation of nuclear war should require East and West to moderate their competition and pursue peaceful coexistence. Nor is it new to argue that nuclear weapons invalidate any idea that war could ever be the continuation of politics.[120] But Gorbachev has used the certainty that nuclear war creates mutual risk for all societies to put "human interests" ahead of "class interests" and set aside East-West rivalry for the long term. Moreover, Gorbachev has emphasized the growing danger of accidental war, or war by computer malfunction. As he has described them, nuclear weapons put the world "in the captivity of technology and of military and technocratic logic,"[121] and a war could break out "uncontrollably" at any time.[122] Thus "anxieties and fears" are a source of insecurity in the nuclear age, and rough parity by itself may not be good enough as a guarantee of national security. Gorbachev has also rejected the idea that nuclear weapons have provided peace: "It seems more correct to say that a world war has been averted despite the existence of these weapons."[123]

As his basic approach to security policy, Gorbachev has emphasized that all must feel equally secure. He has denounced as "absurd and immoral" a situation in which security is built on fear of retribution, but rejects defense against nuclear weapons as hopeless. Thus Gorbachev has urged that the superpowers seek to cut strategic weapons to the lowest possible levels, and follow the principle of "reasonable sufficiency" in weaponry, and "non-offensive defense" in plans and deployments to reduce mutual fears about each other's intentions. At the Party Congress in 1986, Gorbachev linked these ideas in his ambitious proposal for a "comprehensive international security system" based on the United Nations, a system which would eliminate all weapons of mass destruction, ban chemical weapons, disband military alliances, cut all military forces to "reasonable" levels, establish a "new international economic order," and settle regional conflicts.[124]

The question of the sources for policy change in the West is a tricky one. Gorbachev has not hesitated to complain that "U.S. militarism is in the forefront of the forces which threaten mankind with war,"[125] and has charged that the "ruling reactionary upper crust in the U.S." views reduction of East-West tension as a threat to their interests.[126] He has also specifically denied that he is the victim of any illusions that imperialism "has become good:"

> Have imperialist sources of aggression and wars really vanished? No. We are not forgetting the threat to peace from imperialist militarism and we believe that for the moment no guarantees have been provided for the irreversibility of the positive processes that have begun.[127]

As snags emerged in the bilateral arms control negotiations, Gorbachev has argued that U.S. "reactionaries" were trying to perpetuate the arms race, and were hoping that a new competition in strategic defenses would exhaust the USSR economically.[128]

Nonetheless, Gorbachev's approach has been to emphasize that "there are opportunities for curbing the forces of militarism," or blocking "its most dangerous manifestations," provided that a "degree of realism" could permit Western leaders to "see things soberly."[129] Successful conclusion of the INF treaty was taken as evidence that American leaders could take a "sensible, effective stance." Gorbachev has claimed that his arms control initiatives and the INF treaty have helped to change the image of the USSR and undermine "the ideological foundations of anti-Soviet and imperialist policy." Thus the "new political thinking," the new Soviet foreign policy style, readiness for compromise, and rejection of the "ideologization" of interstate relations, along with changes inside Western society and international pressures for peace have produced a gain for the "party of peace" in the United States.[130]

Gorbachev has no apologies for the development of Soviet military strength, which he always describes as logical and necessary for the survival of the state. As he said in his book, *Perestroika*, "we have been under permanent threat of potential aggression" since the Bolshevik revolution. "Try getting in our shoes and see for yourself."[131] He has defended the achievement of strategic parity with the West, and has pledged that his government "will never allow the United States to achieve superiority in nuclear missiles."[132] However, he clearly believes that military strength can become counterproductive, and has referred to "improvident" Soviet actions which fed Western fears.[133] Over and over again Gorbachev has insisted that the USSR's "enemy image" feeds anti-Sovietism and anti-communism.[134] By allowing itself to be drawn into an arms race, the USSR was helping its enemies, not itself. Thus, while he has routinely blamed the West for the arms race, Gorbachev has suggested that the Soviet Union must look to its own behavior, and take some responsibility for convincing others that it is not aggressive. The growth in Soviet military power, and its projection into other countries, are part of the problem. As Gorbachev has said several times, concentration on "the military aspect of confronting imperialism" meant that opportunities were lost for reducing tension. Once the USSR became caught up in the arms race, its stance in favor of peace and disarmament was just not convincing.[135] Gorbachev's new security policy is intended to present a more credible and less threatening face.

Gorbachev's views are expanded upon by some commentators who make the case that it is in fact unlikely the Western alliance would consider attacking the socialist camp.[136] The unilateral Soviet moves have been described as "evidence of confidence that common sense will make headway in international affairs" despite the lack of corresponding actions from the Western side.[137]

Gorbachev, like his predecessors, has indicated that the USSR is quite prepared to do whatever is required to maintain its defenses if U.S. military spending so indicates, whether this means matching levels of offensive weapons or adding forces to offset SDI. As he put it in 1986, "the Soviet Union lays no claim to greater security, but will not settle for less."[138] However, saving money on defense in the interests of domestic reforms is clearly preferable. This has been expressed indirectly in comments aimed at Western audiences which stress that the Soviet Union "needs peace" in order to concentrate on raising its own standard of living.[139] Gorbachev has been equally clear in less public fora that building up arms at the expense of the domestic economy served the interests of the enemy. "Our opponent has made an attempt to impede our socioeconomic development. That is one of the reasons why detente in its time was replaced by a new wave in the Cold War." For this reason Gorbachev stresses that the success of Soviet foreign policy depends on a healthy Soviet society and economy.[140]

The fact that Gorbachev's approach to security policy justifies—even demands—cuts in defense spending has not gone down easily. As he has moved to consolidate his political power it is clear that there has been resistance to his analysis and its implication that East-West tension should be reduced while domestic needs receive budgetary priority.[141] At the Party Congress in 1986, Gorbachev referred to the desirability of "balanced and proportionate reduction of military budgets."[142] In the buildup to the 19th Party Conference in June 1988, the military budget was a conspicuous target. The Theses prepared by the Central Committee expressed the view that Soviet security had been enhanced under Gorbachev "not through a building up of strength but by increasing trust in our country," and included a statement that "primarily qualitative parameters" must apply in managing the Soviet military establishment.[143] At the conference itself, Gorbachev complained publicly about the impact of the arms race on the Soviet economy.[144] Articles by supporters of *perestroika* have called attention to the burden of defense spending on the domestic economy, and praised the use of "political means" to achieve security more cheaply.[145] Shevardnadze's speech to the Foreign Ministry conference in July was even blunter about the costliness of the arms race:

> An enemy can be exhausted and bled white through an arms race, but at the cost of one's own economic and social base being undermined. This conclusion is so obvious that if we sidestep or touch upon it only superficially we will not help strengthen our own security at all.

His reference to "imperialist maneuvering" to draw the USSR into the arms race buttresses arguments that Soviet advocates of high defense spending play into the hands of the enemy. Moreover, Shevardnadze attacked the idea that the Soviet Union should be militarily more powerful than all its potential opponents, and criticized military "imprudence" which can "cost the country dearly." Shevardnadze also had harsh words for the costly choice to pursue acquisition of chemical weapons, a choice which "diverted substantial production capacities, manpower and other resources." The result of this effort, he pointed out, was a stockpile which must be destroyed at additional costs, damage to the Soviet image abroad, and no real gain for national security.[146]

Defense budget figures have still not been fully publicized, despite promises by Gorbachev and complaints from Shevardnadze and others. However in December 1988 Gorbachev's address to the United Nations included an announcement that the USSR would unilaterally reduce its armed forces by half a million men; withdraw troops from Central Europe, European USSR and Mongolia; remove six tank divisions from East Germany, Hungary and Czechoslovakia; and restructure Warsaw Pact units to be "unambiguously defensive." He also offered to submit plans for converting Soviet military industry for civilian use to the UN.[147] During a major review of *perestroika* in January 1989, Gorbachev linked cuts in the military budget to the need for "some fairly sharp and decisive measures" to repair state finances. He claimed that planned cuts (14.2 percent of the operational budget, and 19.5 percent of procurement) could be made "without reducing the level of security and the defense capability of the state."[148]

By February 1989 Gorbachev was boasting that "for the first time in the postwar years and maybe in all history our country's security has been strengthened not because of the escalation of military power and not because of the increase of the already huge defense expenditure," and proudly cited "substantial reduction" of military spending as well as "a partial reconversion of military production" to civilian purposes.[149] The stage is well set for continuation of this line, presuming continued successes for overall Soviet foreign policy.

Regional Conflicts

Actual or potential Soviet military involvement in Third World conflicts has been a major source of East-West tension, and an important factor in the demise of detente. The issue of "regional conflicts" was brought to the agenda of Soviet-American relations by President Reagan, who cited Soviet fighting in Afghanistan, military aid to the Sandinista regime in Nicaragua, support to the Vietnamese-controlled regime in Kampuchea and the Cuban-backed embattled government in Angola as evidence of a need for Western vigilance and rearmament. From the very first Reagan-Gorbachev summit in November, 1985, it was clear that these regional conflicts were an impediment to improvement of East-West relations.

In his report on the Geneva summit, Gorbachev acknowledged that regional conflicts are especially dangerous because of the possibility they could escalate. But he criticized the American view of the conflicts as manifestations of East-West rivalry. Rejecting this "relapse into imperial thinking," Gorbachev claimed that for the most part these conflicts arise from economic and social conditions.[150] When Gorbachev announced the "new political thinking" at the Party Congress in February 1986, "regional conflicts" (meaning primarily Third World conflicts) were again described as products of internal factors—a formulation which minimizes the ideological aspects of these conflicts. He also made headlines by describing the situation in Afghanistan as a "running sore" and announcing that the USSR would like to withdraw its troops "in the very near future," once a settlement was reached that would assure an end to outside armed interference there.[151] Gorbachev also supported the idea of *collective* efforts to "defuse" conflicts "in all the planet's hot spots," and has proposed a greater United Nations role in this regard.[152] In February 1988, Gorbachev announced a political settlement of the war in Afghanistan had been reached in the "proximity talks" in Geneva, and that Soviet troops would be completely withdrawn within one year. He indicated that the Soviet leadership had been looking for a way out of Afghanistan since 1985, and was satisfied that the settlement could assure an independent, neutral, and nonaligned Afghanistan in harmony with Soviet state interests.[153] At the Party Conference in June 1988, Gorbachev referred to the Afghan settlement as "an important international landmark."[154] He has regularly cited the withdrawal as one of the signs that the new political thinking is working, and that international relations are being "transformed" for the better.[155]

Gorbachev's willingness to support settlements of regional conflicts through United Nations auspices (as in the case of Afghanistan) or through American mediation (as in Angola) has required some justification. As it has emerged, the new Soviet "line" on regional conflicts is that they are primarily caused by factors indigenous to the region or the particular regimes involved, that a superpower code of conduct could eliminate external factors which fan such conflicts, and that international mechanisms (especially the United Nations) can be useful in applying political solutions which reconcile warring parties and factions.[156]

As Gorbachev has expressed it, local conflicts "should not engender confrontation between the two systems,"[157] since the dangers of such conflicts affect all states:

> The bell of each regional conflict tolls for all of us. This is particularly true because these conflicts are occurring in the 'Third World' which even without this has many troubles and problems on a scale which cannot fail to concern all of us.[158]

Abandonment of "zero-sum" thinking, concerns about the impact of involvement in regional conflicts on East-West relations, and the reevaluation of the prospects of Third World socialism are all involved in this new approach. Ideological issues concern the solidarity with progressive forces which had been said in the past to require Soviet assistance to liberation struggles. The "new political thinking" draws attention instead to the hazards of such assistance in a nuclear world, given the danger that small conflicts "of whatever sort have a tendency to grow into regional, and even world conflicts." One approach to this dilemma has been to emphasize that the progressive forces should exercise restraint:

> The nuclear age requires that revolutionary forces be extremely circumspect in deciding on armed struggle and that they fundamentally reject the various manifestations of leftist extremism. On the other hand, the nuclear age has by no means removed the necessity of delivering a resolute rebuff to reaction and counterrevolution wherever they attempt to use force to do away with the people's democratic and socialist gains and to turn back the clock of historical progress.[159]

But how is the choice to pursue political, "collective" settlements of ongoing regional conflicts in the Third World to be reconciled with the interest in advances by progressives? Or, as Yevgeni Primakov has put it, "How, under present conditions does the Soviet Union perform its *class mission?*" In his speech at the 19th Party Conference, Primakov gave this answer:

> Mostly (and the extreme importance of this does not require additional explanations) by ruling out war from the life of modern society. If mankind were drawn into an all-embracing thermonuclear catastrophe, none of the national or social liberation movements would have any value.

While Primakov stressed that the USSR has "in no way given up its sympathies or its actual support for the forces of progress and construction" and remains "a firm opponent of any attempts to export counter-revolution to countries where progressive forces have come to power," he insisted that even those whose struggles are justified need to demonstrate a sense of responsibility. Moreover, he suggests that "national reconciliation" settlements in Afghanistan, Kampuchea and Nicaragua for conflicts between governments and indigenous "reactionaries" can work because the superpowers stand to gain by removing and restraining themselves.[160]

The most ardent supporters of *perestroika* have portrayed these settlements as making the best of a bad business. Primakov has criticized the Soviet intervention in Afghanistan as a decision taken "without properly studying the various alternatives of a political settlement," and "without a real understanding of either the situation in Afghanistan or the inevitability of the consequences of the measures taken." The heavy burden this decision created for the Soviet people makes the withdrawal from Afghanistan a real achievement.[161] Dashichev has derided the thinking behind Soviet involvement in Third World conflicts, and blamed it for ruining detente at great cost to domestic interests:

> Though we were politically, militarily (via weapons supplies and advisers) and diplomatically involved in regional conflicts, we disregarded their influence on the relaxation of tension between the USSR and the West and on their entire system of relationships. There were no clear ideas of the Soviet Union's true national state interests. These interests lay by no means in chasing petty and essentially formal gains associated with leadership coups in certain developing countries.[162]

Others have voiced similar complaints: "Our direct or indirect entanglement in regional conflicts brings about enormous losses, exacerbating overall international tensions, justifying the arms race and hampering mutually beneficial economic ties with the West."[163]

A recent article by the Deputy Director of the Africa Institute has described a "vicious circle" of relationships between the superpowers and Third World conflicts: their rivalry draws them in, but intensifies both the conflicts and the rivalry. Thus these conflicts represent the worst example of the hazards of "zero-sum" thinking:

> If we see the world as divided into hostile blocs which are constantly building up their arms, it is also natural to view regional conflicts through the prism of confrontation: 'Whose side are you on?' . . . The logic of this approach dictates the need to 'score points' in global confrontation and to regard a loss for the other side as a 'gain' for your own side. . . . By observing a balance of interests, the gain of the other side certainly need not entail loss for yourself, and vice versa.

This scholar recommended that both the USSR and the United States exercise "reasonable restraint" to inhibit the escalation of regional conflicts. He described the export of arms to Third World states as "primarily a political act," so that "political will" would be required to shut off these arms, but apparently expected the lessons of history to be persuasive. He pointed out that weapons shipments have not necessarily created reliable allies, nor have regional conflicts ended in clear victories.[164]

Self-Image and Imperial Presence

Disaffection with Soviet commitments to Third World socialists did not begin with Mikhail Gorbachev. It was expressed at the highest level by Gorbachev's patron, Yuri Andropov, in a statement in 1983 whose key phrases have been incorporated into the new Party Program:

> It is one thing to proclaim socialism as a goal, and another to build it. For this, a certain level of productive forces, culture, and social consciousness are needed. Socialist countries express solidarity with these progressive states, render assistance to them in the sphere of politics and culture, and cooperate with them in strengthening their defense. We contribute also, to the extent of our capabilities, to their economic development. But basically, as with social progress as a whole, this can of course only be the result of the work of their peoples, and a correct policy of their leadership.[165]

Gorbachev's downgrading of ideology has brought with it both indirect and direct distancing from socialist governments and anti-imperialist causes in the Third World. At the 27th Party Congress, Gorbachev's few references to the Third World lacked the enthusiasm of earlier leadership statements for "consolidation of the alliance of world socialism and the national-liberation movement."[166] He neither sang the praises of the USSR's socialist oriented allies, nor pledged support for their cause. The developing countries were referred to as a group, whose distressing condition was cited as "the true source" of many regional conflicts. A reference to the "slow, arduous but unstoppable process of socioeconomic transformation" did not single out socialist oriented countries for any special plaudits, and noted that these states were encountering "considerable difficulties." The section of his speech outlining principles and goals of Soviet foreign policy mentioned the Third World only in the context of a call for "collective international action" to resolve regional conflicts there, and in a general statement of solidarity with "the forces of national and social liberation" and close interaction with socialist oriented countries, revolutionary-democratic parties, and the nonaligned movement. The "export of counter-revolution" (a euphemism for Western military involvement in the Third World generally used to defend Soviet military involvement) was mentioned only as an example of international terrorism in a list which included hijackings and political assassinations.[167]

The chapter on the Third World in *Perestroika* included statements of support for the "national liberation struggle of African nations;" sympathy with "nations fighting for freedom and independence," and dedication to the right of all states to choose their path of development. However, the focus was on the general problems of development, debt, local conflicts, regional security issues, and the ways in which reduced East-West tension could contribute to progress in solving them.[168] In his November revolutionary anniversary speech in 1987, despite a nod to the contribution of revolutionary regimes to "intensification of political energy" in the Third World, Gorbachev's main thrust was to warn the West about treating all these countries unfairly. He acknowledged a decline in the national liberation movement as natural for the times, and cited the vigor of assertiveness by regional organizations like the Organization of African Unity, League of Arab States, and the Association of South East Asian Nations.[169] Thesis No. 10 on foreign policy prepared for the June 1988 Party Conference did not mention the Third World at all; nor did Gorbachev's speech to the Conference, despite a statement about the importance of "free choice of path" and condemnation of the forceful imposition of social systems by outsiders.[170]

Gorbachev's disinterest in Third World causes has built on an established mood of disillusionment with the USSR's commitments there, and the "de-ideologizing" of interstate relations has encouraged some significant revision of the theoretical foundations of Soviet involvement.[171]

In his call for rethinking world politics., Gorbachev noted that "the young independent states" face difficult problems. Together with other "new realities" this demands "an ability to rethink many things, and demands a bold, creative approach."[172] For some Soviet scholars of Third World development, this was an invitation to "tell the truth" about the real achievements of socialist oriented regimes. The dismal economic performance of the Marxist-Leninist states, compared with the impressive levels achieved by some capitalist oriented Third World states brings into question the old theory that backward countries can—and should move toward socialism.[173] This new realism has also involved admissions that even those Third World countries which are members of the socialist camp—including Cuba, Vietnam and Mongolia—have not been particularly successful in their development strategies.[174]

As Soviet scholars have become more critical of their own developmental path, and the way in which accelerated development was pursued in the nineteen thirties, they have rethought the wisdom of recommending that Third World states try to make an even greater "leap" toward socialism. An overpowerful bureaucracy has been blamed for "distorting" the USSR's development by disregarding economic realities and ignoring poor performance. This has been understood by many scholars to warn that Third World countries which choose socialism and attempt to reshape their economies from above inevitably face even greater temptations to create bureaucratic authorities which will undermine their aspirations. For some, this is sufficient reason to challenge the theory that a noncapitalist path to socialism is available to the Third World.[175]

> The more critical we are of our own experience, the more it is evident we must make corresponding correctives of doctrine in our assessments of the nature of the period of transition to socialism in the developing countries of the Orient.[176]

Attacks on "wishful thinking" and examination of the realities which show that little real progress has been made toward socialism even in the most committed Third World states undermine the theoretical base for the Soviet political and military offensive in the developing world. One Soviet scholar has caustically complained that had his superiors in the Academy of Science displayed less foolish optimism and paid more attention to scholarly doubts about Marxist-Leninist revolutions in backward countries, the invasion of Afghanistan could have been avoided.[177]

The poor performance of socialist-oriented Third World states has made them a drain on the Soviet Union, as well as an embarrassment. The domestic priority of *perestroika* has been reflected in observations by some Soviet scholars that the emergence of more socialist-oriented states might not be in the national interest.[178] Others have complained about the economic burden these countries represent,[179] and Shevardnadze has recently warned that aid and assistance to developing countries will have to fall.[180]

The most blistering criticism of Soviet Third World policy has been in relation to military involvement, in keeping with the theme that foreign policy should serve Soviet national interests, and that stereotypes and preoccupation with class struggle should not encourage confrontation in an "interdependent but integral world." Dashichev pounced on efforts to spread socialism to countries "totally unprepared" for it, efforts he described as "chasing petty and essentially formal gains associated with leadership coups in certain developing countries."[181] Foreign Ministry official Kozyrev took a similar line, complaining that militant and "ultra-progressive" rhetoric of Third World radicals has not been matched by actual social and public policies. In fact, he blamed poor domestic performance and undemocratic practices in these states for conflicts with indigenous political opposition movements—a picture of regional conflicts squarely in line with the idea that political settlements and "national reconciliation" are appropriate and urgent. Kozyrev also directly challenged what he called the "myth" that the developing countries and the USSR share a commitment to anti-imperialism:

> First, the majority of developing countries are already professing, or leaning to, the Western model of development and they are suffering not so much from capitalism as from its shortage, and second, they are interested not in confrontation with their former mother countries, but in cooperation in safeguarding their own and international stability, which should be the goal of our cooperation with the Third World.

On this basis, he questioned whether a "class alliance" with Third World anti-imperialists was worth the risk of confrontation with the West.[182]

Soviet scholars are not unanimous in their eagerness to abandon the socialist cause in Third World circumstances. Several have protested the "new thinking" insofar as it appears to give up on socialism, and to say that developing countries must suffer through capitalist development.[183] Nonetheless the most enthusiastic of Gorbachev's supporters have gone further, to suggest that the West is not completely committed to exploitation of the Third World, and that "some elements" within the advanced capitalist countries are actually prepared for positive cooperation with the Third World states.[184] Thus the new world view helps to erode the ideological foundations for an activist and interventionist policy in the Third World.

Prospects for Gorbachev's Secular Outlook

Gorbachev has said that ideology should be removed from inter*state* relations, although not from inter*national* relations. Ideological differences and the conflicts they engender are the objects of his criticism. Clearly, Gorbachev believes that a focus on ideological differences has hurt Soviet interests, and that ideological thinking has impaired foreign policy decision making. His critique is a profound one, but there are many reasons for doubting that it will be a lasting one.

Ideology serves several functions for Soviet foreign policy. The most basic of these is an interpretive one. Marxism-Leninism is a theory which presumes that societies are moving toward a better future through dialectical struggles between advanced and regressive forces. Given this broad picture, communists expect to use ideological categories to derive an analysis of the dynamics of world affairs at any particular point. These ideologically derived interpretations of international politics should identify important trends, significant motive forces, and the status of socioeconomic developments. The presumption of struggle has historically focused attention on the need to provide analyses of the current intensity of the struggle, the source of present dangers, identification of appropriate resources and allies, and tactical prescriptions for success and survival. The Manichean nature of the Marxist-Leninist world view has made this interpretive function seem an urgent and very important one. However, there is nothing predetermined about these interpretations. Over time, official determinations of the pace of progress and the intensity of the struggle have varied considerably, from near-paranoia to confident optimism.

The ideology's vision of a communist social future as the historical destination of humankind has in a certain sense supplied a basic motive or ultimate goal for Soviet foreign policy. However, the operational meaning of this ideal has varied. The young Soviet state quickly abandoned the view that it had an obligation to promote world revolution with its armies. Under Stalin, the doctrine of "socialism in one country" substituted concern for the strength and safety of the USSR for crude messianism. Khrushchev painted a confident picture about the imminence of socialist triumph, but found that reaching out to establish links with anti-Western revolutionary regimes carried risks. Under Brezhnev, Soviet presence and formidable Soviet military power generated tensions which undermined the temporary stabilization achieved through an East-West strategic military balance.

Perhaps it is most useful to concentrate on the way in which the ideology provides a heroic role for the Soviet Union as the champion of history and vanguard of the future. Whatever the foreign policy posture of the day, Soviet propaganda has endlessly promoted the idea of the USSR as the defender of social justice, the bearer of hope for a better world, and a bulwark of all those oppressed by capitalism and other evil forces. The Soviets have by no means been consistent or selfless supporters of revolutionary movements, but they have sought to portray themselves as both arbiter and leader of the only true international revolutionary movement.

The ideology has also served to provide categories of analysis and tools for thinking about world events. The nature of the ideology has given special importance to determinations about allies and enemies, assessments of danger, evaluations of relative progress, and prospects for favorable change and movement. Such determinations have played an important part in domestic politics. The perception of encirclement by hostile enemies was a crucial element of the rationale for Stalin's authoritarianism, and references to external threats have regularly been used to bolster party rule and justify tight controls over society. In a similar way, Soviet links with the struggles of progressive forces in other countries and support to successful revolutionaries helps to confirm the country's Marxist-Leninist identity as an instrument of progress, and to validate the leadership's purposeful uses of power.

What makes Gorbachev's approach to the ideology of Soviet foreign policy so interesting is that he is doing much more than revising the official interpretation of the external environment. As the previous sections have shown, he essentially claims that the ideology is detrimental to Soviet interests because of the interpretations it supports. Gorbachev does not say directly that the ideology is incorrect, but he advocates that it should be regarded as irrelevant or inappropriate for interstate relations *under current circumstances.* Yet he has altered so many doctrines, and questioned so many accepted ideas about how to find one's way in world affairs, that it is difficult to avoid the conclusion that the overall impact of his approach is destructive of the ideology and its capacity to fulfill its historic functions.

Gorbachev has obviously been highly motivated in both domestic and foreign policy to eliminate restraints which might derive from old ideas about how things must be understood. But his attack on the ideology is also specific: a Manichean world outlook is counterproductive. For Gorbachev, ideology is in the way to the extent that it supports, encourages, or is presumed to require confrontational, aggressive, or belligerent postures and policies. Gorbachev appears convinced of the power of perceptions. While he appreciates that Soviet fears of the West really were justified in the past, he is more concerned about Western fears of the Soviet Union today. He describes these Western fears as understandable ones, given threatening Soviet attitudes and provocative statements. Gorbachev seeks to eliminate the negative impact of the ideology on others—first by disavowing its relevance for East-West relations, and second by building on this disavowal to take actions to dispel some of the concrete sources of Western apprehension.

Gorbachev's critique is intensely practical. Over and over again it has been clear that he believes that ideological categories, dogmas, and conservative habits of thought have driven Soviet foreign policy in unproductive directions. While Gorbachev certainly has not rejected the overall understanding that socialism is the superior social system, he has been willing to abandon wishful thinking about the Soviet role in world politics. Admitting the USSR's economic and social failings is an important justification for *perestroika,* but also serves to discredit boasts that the Soviets are in the lead of an irresistible progressive movement. This kind of "realism" supports an understanding of the Soviet Union as a state preoccupied with domestic difficulties, uninterested in foreign adventures, and no threat to others.

Apocalyptic interpretations of *perestroika* are possible. Indeed, *perestroika* is based on acknowledgment of failure, an indictment of established institutions, and candor about the scale of the problems that must be overcome. But honest self-appraisal may not be as corrosive as some think, for hypocrisy and false promises are old news in the Soviet system. Gorbachev calls for exposure of the truth about the system's performance in order to mobilize for real improvements in the economy and the standard of living. To be sure, his willingness to discard methods and principles previously regarded as sacrosanct erodes a sense of certainty and his emphasis on performance threatens those in comfortable positions and challenges accepted verities about criteria for assessing social values. However, it is also possible to argue that the attack on socioeconomic instrumentalities in defense of basic socialist values, and the reorientation of political and economic management toward better outcomes for the Soviet citizen is an inspiring and fundamentally ideological movement. Such a judgment would depend on one's definition of socialism, of course. Thus Gorbachev's reforms can be seen as an attempt to redefine socialism operationally with an emphasis on raising living standards and increasing societal productivity, rather than on eliminating exploitation.

It is possible to argue that the erosion of ideological doctrines in domestic life and in foreign policy are parallel and mutually reinforcing developments. That is, it may be that a less distinctively socialist foreign policy is a natural outgrowth of less distinctively socialist economic doctrines. Certainly a similar iconoclastic spirit informs both, and the fates of *perestroika* and the new political thinking about foreign affairs seem inevitably linked. This may mean that the new attitude toward ideology and foreign policy cannot survive domestic economic setbacks.

Considered independently, however, there are several ways in which Gorbachev's approach to ideological aspects of foreign policy is vulnerable. For one thing, there are some tensions inherent in his positions. For instance, at the same time that Gorbachev seeks to divert attention from excessively confrontational attitudes toward the West, his emphasis on domestic renewal derives from acutely competitive impulses. *Perestroika* aims not just to repair the Soviet system, but to improve socialism's image, prestige and performance relative to that of capitalism. For the moment, Gorbachev has tried to deflect attention from capitalist-socialist antagonisms to the "global issues" and "universal values" that all peoples share. He denies that his heavy borrowing from capitalist economic practice, and his abandonment of some cherished, distinctively "socialist" techniques will have the effect of blurring distinctions between the two systems or promote their "convergence." But whether or not the end result will be "socialist" or not, the aim is still to "catch up" with the most advanced Western states, and to earn the leadership position the first socialist state should by rights enjoy.

The loss of ideological messianism may also be a serious vulnerability. Marxist-Leninist ideology has provided an international identity for the USSR as champion of the good, challenger of the old and evil. Gorbachev advocates giving up this role because it is dangerous and expensive, but also because the Soviet Union is not an attractive leader, and because the cause it embodies is not popular or powerful right now. Overall, Gorbachev proposes to change the measures of success for the Soviet Union as an international actor. World politics is depicted not as a battlefield or testing ground, but a marketplace with competitive standards the Soviets must work hard to meet. Promoting the expansion of friendly relations with all sorts of states, full participation in the international economy, and open exchanges with all cultures leaves little room for heroics—unless we consider Gorbachev's brand of vocal environmentalism as heroic. Gorbachev proposes to remove not only class struggle, but a class identity. The image of the USSR as the headquarters of a distinctive, separate and superior political and economic system may never have been accurate, but it has offered comfort and provided a basic orientation toward events and actors in the world arena for a long time. To the extent we have heard Gorbachev's domestic critics clearly, it seems they are very disturbed about erosion of this identity, and this distinctiveness.

Where Marxist-Leninist views of world politics have traditionally seen a two-sided battle of contending social forces, in which the USSR was on the preponderant side expected to emerge victorious, Gorbachev suggests a need to focus on balancing interests. Moreover, he has taken pains to explain that all states have legitimate interests which will necessarily be in conflict, but which can be managed through mutual respect. This amounts to a call for tolerance toward the needs and demands of other states which violates decades of thinking in which state interests were not regarded as "neutral," but as reflecting the interests of profoundly different and incompatible groups.

Another vulnerability in Gorbachev's views lies in his attitude toward power. Gorbachev explicitly recommends a change in Soviet thinking about the sources of security, based on a recognition of the impossibility of relying on military force any longer. However, Gorbachev gives little credit to the USSR's accumulated military might. This is in sharp contrast to his predecessors, for whom the achievement of strategic parity was a source of pride and considerable comfort. To Gorbachev, this military power represents a problem and a source of insecurity. He makes this argument on both military and political grounds. He asserts first of all that existing nuclear stockpiles are so large that an East-West conflict would be intolerably destructive. Moreover, he has warned that computer-controlled technologically sophisticated weapons are unacceptably susceptible to accidental use. At the same time, political tensions contribute to a competitive arms race which has a life of its own, and generates increasingly intolerable levels of military spending on both sides. This arms race, in turn, sustains the kind of tensions that can cause a war. Ideology contributes to this situation to the extent it supports assumptions of perpetual, irreconcilable hostility between the opposing social systems.

Of course the dilemma in this analysis is that a successful policy of reducing tension would remove the incentive to avoid conflict. In fact, how risky is it for East and West to compete? Once the risk of war seems sufficiently remote, of what value is an ardent commitment to tension reduction? It seems that it is precisely the emphasis on the danger of global thermonuclear war that is the weakest link of Gorbachev's reasoning. If the danger of nuclear war justifies "humanizing" international relations, giving up military instruments and seeking dialogue in an international context to resolve conflicts that could otherwise escalate, what will happen once the process of dialogue and peaceful conflict resolution are underway? With every step toward the kind of "de-ideologized" interstate relations Gorbachev has described, the fear of nuclear war which drives this movement would seem to become less relevant and less powerful.

Moreover, Gorbachev's policies presume Western reasonableness—which must come either from similar fears of nuclear war, or from popular pressure in favor of less confrontational East-West relations. There is plenty of evidence to suggest that the Soviet leadership is not uniformly sanguine in its views of Western governments. Some have questioned the assumption that capitalist countries will be sufficiently impressed by the danger of war to assign the highest priority to "human values." For example, a writer in a military journal recently warned that "the threat of war is not obsolete," and cited a George Bush statement that the Cold War is not over.[185] Others have been skeptical about the actual response from the West to Soviet concessions.[186] A few have warned that fear of nuclear war actually benefits the "imperialists."[187] Nor is it clear whether Western actions can ever completely match the demands Soviets may set for "reasonableness."

Another vulnerability concerns the lack of positive vision. Marxism-Leninism cannot be reduced to one tenet; nonetheless its theory of dialectical struggle leading to social progress provides a central teleology. While Gorbachev may not have abandoned the idea that socialism will ultimately triumph, he prefers to focus on the need to address socialism's current shortcomings. He has stressed that several efforts to achieve socialism may be necessary, admits that the contours of an efficient and productive socialist society are still dim, and offers neither a timetable nor a destination. Similarly, his views encourage admissions that the USSR has no guaranteed model for developing countries, and may need to abandon the idea of assisting backward peoples to find an exploitation-free path to modernization. This lack of certainty about the direction and aims of Soviet policy may represent a long-overdue realism, but may also prove to weaken the authority of the leadership.

Ultimately Gorbachev's changes of emphasis in ideological matters are linked to his understanding of contemporary problems, and to his current foreign policy agenda. Should this analysis change, or this agenda change, the view of the relevance of ideology to East-West relations could change too. Certainly if Gorbachev himself were to be replaced, this would provide an opportunity for a new leadership to redefine priorities. It is also worth noticing that a state need not have a Manichean outlook or a highly articulated ideology to pursue an imperial policy. An equation of Soviet national interest with Marxism-

Leninism is, of course, an old tradition, easily asserted no matter what the particular content of Marxism-Leninism.

Gorbachev's revisions of ideology will appeal to the pragmatists and reformers, but will almost certainly disturb those within the USSR who associate ideological stability with legitimacy, order and stability. Thus the fact that the new political thinking reduces the distinctiveness and the missionary quality of Soviet foreign policy may be a serious liability. Yet it is difficult to be sure how unsettling Gorbachev's revisions may prove to be (or whether they must be as unsettling as many Western analysts believe). So far, Gorbachev's revisions already have the character of a new orthodoxy which has been effectively enforced. The periodic introduction of a new set of precepts and principles in foreign policy is a familiar process within the Soviet Union, and does not rule out a shift to a different set should circumstances or leaders change.

Gorbachev has boasted about the successes of his foreign policy initiatives, and the net reduction in the danger of war which he says has been accomplished. However, the position and status of the USSR after this reduction of tension may not satisfy Soviet pride. Gorbachev has identified regional conflicts as dangerous to the extent they become ideologized—that is, to the extent they take on East-West aspects. But a fear of escalation to nuclear war may not be justified in all cases of regional conflict. Moreover, the political outcome of the settlements reached is still uncertain, and may not be viewed as sufficiently favorable to the Soviet Union. There may also come a time when Gorbachev's stance will change (or be rejected), should some of the USSR's allies become threatened or should the West be involved in some local war.

One way to interpret Gorbachev's new approach is as a "diplomacy of decline"[188]—a redefinition of the world which accepts limits, rationalizes lower expectations, reinterprets the international environment as less threatening and recasts goals downward to more moderate and more attainable dimensions. Certainly this is one impact of public admissions that the USSR has little "attractive force" for others because of its poor standard of life compared with the advanced Western states. In the past Soviet deficits were blamed on hostile Western encirclement; now the Soviet people are told they are themselves to blame for their decline. This is an uncomfortable reinterpretation. And should the West abandon its fear and suspicion of the Soviet Union, it might be precisely at that time that a Soviet leadership would be tempted to revise its view of the international scene in ways which would justify renewed Soviet aggressiveness to improve its position relative to a newly quiescent adversary.

It can always be argued that ideological argumentation is secondary, and that great power ambitions will continue to be the source of the most troublesome Soviet policies abroad. This is another way of saying that while the ideological changes described in this paper may not be meaningless, their independent effects on Soviet foreign policy are less important for us than the Soviet leadership's understanding of foreign policy priorities at any given time. At the present time, Gorbachev's priority is the reduction of East-West tension in order to permit a shift of attention and resources to domestic reforms. Tension reduction secondarily serves to support increased trade and contact with other societies, all of which should assist and support the reconstruction of the Soviet economy. The interest in arms control and in settlement of regional conflicts both derive from this focus. However, once East-West tension is reduced, the policy priorities are less obvious, and the rationale for setting aside philosophical differences would seem less acute.

Reducing Western fears and improving the Soviet image appear to solve public relations problems, but may not be perceived as yielding enough tangible benefits to be persuasive priorities. Moreover, the new political thinking in foreign policy has become associated with greater openness to new ideas and with the flourishing of many social novelties. The social and political ferment such openness has produced within the Soviet society and federal state may indirectly work to discredit Gorbachev's foreign policy.

Gorbachev's desire to remove ideology from interstate relations supports a unique and serious reorientation of Soviet foreign policy. This reorientation may prove fragile, but it may be some time before we can be sure. Both external and internal developments may be expected to shape the future evolution of Gorbachev's views and the foreign policy priorities they serve.

Notes

1. Gorbachev speech to the April 1985 Central Committee Plenum, in Mikhail Gorbachev, *Selected Speeches and Articles* (Moscow: Progress, 1987), pp. 14, 15, 18.
2. *Ibid.*, p. 15.
3. Gorbachev's Report for the Central Committee to the 27th Party Congress, *Pravda*, February 26, 1986, in *Foreign Broadcast Information Service Daily Report* (FBIS) March 28, 1986. (Extracted in Document No. 1, Part Two.)
4. *Pravda*, February 18, 1988, in FBIS February 19, 1988. (Extracted in Document No. 4, Part Two.)
5. Thesis No. 2 of ten submitted to the Extraordinary Party Conference of June, 1988, *Pravda*, 27 May, 1988, in FBIS May 27, 1988.
6. *Pravda*, February 18, 1988, in FBIS February 19, 1988. (Extracted in Document No. 4, Part Two.)
7. In October 1988, Yegor Ligachev, the Politburo member who has publicly contradicted some of Gorbachev's statements, was shifted from responsibility for ideology and party personnel to head the new Central Committee Commission on Agriculture. Ligachev is known to be critical of policies which might weaken the collectivized farm system; but being responsible for agriculture could also make him and his more conservative approach vulnerable should food supply problems not be resolved soon.
8. *Pravda*, February 26, 1986, in FBIS March 28, 1986. (Extracted in Document No. 1, Part Two.)
9. Mikhail Gorbachev, *Perestroika: New Thinking for Our Country and the World* (New York: Harper and Row, 1987), p. 105.
10. *Perestroika*, p. 21.
11. *Pravda*, February 26, 1986, in FBIS March 28, 1986. (Extracted in Document No. 1, Part Two.)
12. Gorbachev's concluding remarks to the 27th party Congress, March 6, 1986, in Gorbachev, *Selected Speeches and Articles*, pp. 463–64.
13. Speech to the April 23, 1985 Central Committee Plenum; in Gorbachev, *Selected Speeches and Articles*, pp. 28, 11.
14. *Pravda*, February 26, 1986, in FBIS March 28, 1986. (Extracted in Document No. 1, Part Two.)
15. *Perestroika*, p. 45.
16. Gorbachev's revolutionary anniversary speech of November 2, 1987 on Moscow television, in FBIS November 3, 1987. (Extracted in Document No. 2, Part Two.)

17. *Literaturnaia Rossiia,* June 17, 1988; in *Joint Publications Research Service Report* (JPRS) UPA-88-032, August 16, 1988, p. 15.
18. *Pravda,* February 26, 1986, in FBIS March 28, 1986. (Extracted in Document No. 1, Part Two.)
19. Gorbachev's concluding remarks to the 27th party Congress, in Gorbachev, *Selected Speeches and Articles,* pp. 463-64. A philosopher named Furmanov has gone further, with a criticism of "institutionalized dogmatism" under Stalin. *Sovetskaia Kultura,* March 12, 1988, in FBIS May 24, 1988.
20. *Perestroika,* pp. 50, 26.
21. *Pravda,* April 23, 1988, in FBIS April 25, 1988.
22. *Pravda,* June 26, 1987, in FBIS June 26, 1987.
23. *Kommunist,* No. 17, 1988, in FBIS Feb 3, 1989.
24. *Pravda,* June 26, 1987, in FBIS June 26, 1987; and *Pravda,* June 29, 1988. See also "Ideologiia revoliutsionnoi mysli i deistviia," *Kommunist,* No. 5, 1988, 3-11, p. 4, which calls for a purge of "anything that has prevented realization of socialism's potential;" and V. Il'in and A. Razumov, "Dogmatizm teorii—defitsit otvetstvennosti," *Kommunist,* No. 12, 1988, pp. 60-72.
25. *Pravda,* June 26, 1987, in FBIS June 26, 1987.
26. *Ibid.;* his speech in Krasnoyarsk of September 18, 1988, in FBIS September 20, 1988; and his speech in Kiev, *Krasnaia Zvezda,* February 24, 1989, in FBIS February 24, 1989 (extracted in Document No. 10, Part Two).
27. Gorbachev speech at the agriculture plenum, *Pravda,* March 16, 1989, in FBIS March 17, 1989.
28. Gorbachev speech in Kiev, *Krasnaia Zvezda,* February 24, 1989, in FBIS February 24, 1989. (Extracted in Document No. 10, Part Two.)
29. Gorbachev final remarks to a Central Committe conference with Soviet media executives, *Pravda,* May 11, 1-2; in *Current Digest of the Soviet Press* (CDSP), Vol XL, No. 19, 1988, 2-8, 24; p. 8.
30. *Pravda,* February 19, 1988, in FBIS February 19, 1988. (Extracted in Document No. 4, Part Two.)
31. Gorbachev's report to the 19th All-Union CPSU Conference, Moscow Television Service, June 28, 1988, in FBIS June 29, 1988. (Extracted in Document No. 8, Part Two.)
32. Closing remarks at meeting of scientists and cultural figures, *Pravda,* January 8, 1989, in FBIS January 9, 1989.
33. *Krasnaia Zvezda,* February 24, 1989, in FBIS February 24, 1989. (Extracted in Document No. 10, Part Two.)
34. Gorbachev speech in Cuba, in FBIS April 5, 1989.
35. See Gorbachev's speech to the British parliament, *Pravda,* December 19, 1984; his address on French television, September 30, 1985, in *Gorbachev: Selected Speeches and Articles,* p. 198; his October 3, 1985 meeting with members of the French parliament, in *ibid.,* p. 214; and an interview in *Time,* September 9, 1985.
36. Gorbachev at the Ministry of Foreign Affairs in May, 1986, reported in *Vestnik Ministerstva Inostrannykh Del SSSR,* No. 1, 1987, pp. 4-6, in FBIS September 2, 1987.

37. *Ibid.*
38. *Vestnik Ministerstva Inostrannykh Del,* No. 2, 1987, in FBIS October 27, 1987.
39. *Pravda,* February 26, 1986, in FBIS March 28, 1986. (Extracted in Document No. 1, Part Two.)
40. Thesis No. 10, which deals with foreign policy, of ten theses prepared by the Central Committee for submission to the Extraordinary 19th CPSU Conference in 1988, *Pravda,* May 27, 1988, in FBIS May 27, 1988 (Document No. 7, Part Two); and Resolution of the Congress of People's Deputies on Basic Guidelines for Domestic and Foreign Policy of the USSR, *Pravda,* June 25, 1989, in FBIS June 26, 1989.
41. *Pravda,* February 26, 1986, in FBIS March 28, 1986 (extracted in Document No. 1, Part Two). See also *Perestroika,* p. 254, and Thesis No. 10.
42. *Perestroika,* p. 250.
43. Gorbachev speech in Kiev, *Krasnaia Zvezda,* February 24, 1989, in FBIS February 24, 1989 (extracted in Document No. 10, Part Two). Georgi Arbatov has made similar observations: "For a long time we saw [the world] split into two hostile and opposing camps—capitalist and socialist. It was thought in the USSR that an irreconcilable struggle between them would determine the main direction of the world's development. The reality turned out to be much more complex than this scheme although an irreconcilable strife, alas, did for many years, poison East-West relations. The scheme was incorrect because it transferred, mechanically and with oversimplification, the laws of internal development to international relations. At the same time the more important features of the modern epoch were ignored. Today we see the world differently and think that it is one." (*Moscow News,* No. 39, 2–9 October, 1988, JPRS-UIA-88-017, October 28, 1988.) See also Georgi Mirski, *Pravda,* January 25, 1989, in FBIS January 26, 1989: "The idea that it is only 'them' and 'us' in the world and that the struggle must be resolved solely on the basis of the uncompromising principles of 'Who will win?' took shape [in conditions of capitalist encirclement and struggle for survival]."
44. Anatoli Adamishin, "Humanity's Common Destiny," *International Affairs,* No. 2, 1989, p. 3.
45. Gorbachev took up this theme during his visit to France in 1985. See Gorbachev, *Selected Speeches and Articles,* pp. 195, 227. See also Gorbachev's speech to the British parliament in 1984, *Pravda,* December 19, 1984, in CDSP, Vol. 36, No. 51, pp. 2–5.
46. Gorbachev to the April, 1985 Central Committee Plenum, in Gorbachev, *Selected Speeches and Articles,* pp. 11–36; p. 30.
47. Speech to French members of parliament, October 3, 1985, in *Selected Speeches and Articles,* p. 215.
48. April 1985 plenum speech in *Selected Speeches and Articles,* p. 34.
49. *Ibid.,* p. 33.
50. *Ibid.,* pp. 31; 30.
51. *Ibid.,* p. 30.

52. *Pravda,* October 26, 1985, in FBIS October 28, 1985, Supplement, pp. 8, 25, 26. The final program may be found in CDSP, Special Supplement, December 1986.
53. *Pravda,* February 26, 1986, in FBIS March 28, 1986. (Extracted in Document No. 1, Part Two.)
54. *Perestroika,* p. 143.
55. *Pravda,* December 8, 1988, in FBIS December 8, 1988 (extracted in Document No. 9, Part Two); and *Pravda,* January 7, 1989, in FBIS January 9, 1989.
56. Speech to mark Lenin's birthday, April 22, 1983, in Mikhail S. Gorbachev, *A Time for Peace,* (New York: Richardson and Steirman, 1985), p. 23.
57. *Pravda,* February 26, 1986, in FBIS March 28, 1986. (Extracted in Document No. 1, Part Two.)
58. *Perestroika,* pp. 146-148.
59. *Ibid.,* p. 221; Statement to the Press in Geneva (1985), Gorbachev, *Selected Speeches and Articles,* p. 267; and *Pravda,* February 26, 1986, in FBIS March 28, 1986 (extracted in Document No. 1, Part Two).
60. *Pravda,* December 8, 1988, in FBIS December 8, 1988. (Extracted in Document No. 9, Part Two.)
61. Andrei Kozyrev (a Deputy Department Director within the Ministry of Foreign Affairs), "Confidence and the Balance of Interests," *International Affairs,* No. 11, 1988, pp. 3-12.
62. Yuri Zhukov, *Pravda,* March 20, 1989, in FBIS March 23, 1989.
63. Boris Kurashvili, *Moscow News,* June 5, 1988, in FBIS June 27, 1988. See also V. Medvedev, "Velikii oktiabr i sovremennyi mir," *Kommunist,* No. 10, 1988, pp. 3-18, p. 7.
64. *Perestroika,* p. 146.
65. Speech in Kiev, *Krasnaia Zvezda,* February 24, 1989, in FBIS February 24, 1989. (Extracted in Document No. 10, Part Two.)
66. *Perestroika,* pp. 145-147.
67. See Yu. Molchanov, "True to Lenin's Legacy," *International Affairs,* No. 5, 1987, p. 15, E. Pozdniakova, "Natsional'nye, gosydarstvennye i klassovye interesy v mezhdunarodnykh otnosheniiakh," *Mirovaia Ekonomika i Mezhdunarodnye Otnosheniia,* No. 5, 1988, pp. 3-17 and a recent discussion by Yuri Zhukov, *Pravda,* March 20, 1989, in FBIS March 23, 1989. Citations are to V. I. Lenin, *Pol'noe sobranie sochinenii,* Vol. 4, p. 220, and Vol. 30, pp. 43, 44-45.
68. Moscow television November 2, 1987, in FBIS November 3, 1987. (Extracted in Document No. 2, Part Two.) This speech also held back from a full attack on Stalin, and can be viewed as reflecting a compromise with the conservatives.
69. Moscow television, November 4, 1987, in FBIS November 4, 1987. (Extracted in Document No. 3, Part Two.) Anatolii Dobrynin had called upon communists to "interlace" general human and class tasks in a speech in June. (*Pravda,* June 30, 1987, in FBIS July 14, 1987.)
70. *Pravda,* February 19, 1988, in FBIS February 19, 1988. (Extracted in Document No. 4, Part Two.)

71. Moscow Television Service, June 28, 1988, in FBIS June 29, 1988. (Extracted in Document No. 8, Part Two.)
72. *Pravda,* December 8, 1988, in FBIS December 8, 1988. (Extracted in Document No. 9, Part Two.)
73. *Pravda,* January 8, 1989, in FBIS January 9, 1989.
74. S. L. Tikhvinskii, *Novaia i Noveishaia Istoriia,* No. 2, 1988, in JPRS-UPA-88-020, June 6, 1988; E. Pozdniakova, "Natsional'nye, gosydarstvennye i klassovye interesy v mezhdunaroanykh otnosheniiakh;" G. Diligenskii, "Mnenie redaktora: O pol'ze iasnosti," *Mirovaia Ekonomika i Mezdhunarodnye Otnosheniia,* No. 6, 1988, pp. 55–57; and I. Usachev, "Obshchechelovecheskoe i klassovoe v mirovoi politike," *Kommunist,* No. 11, 1988, pp. 109–118.
75. *Perestroika,* p. 147.
76. Jan Triska, ed., *Soviet Communism: Programs and Rules* (San Francisco: Chandler, 1962), p. 66, 65.
77. *Perestroika,* p. 147–148.
78. Medvedev interview, *Kommunist,* No. 17, 1988, in FBIS February 3, 1989.
79. G. Diligenskii, "Mnenie redaktora: O pol'ze iasnosti," and I. Usachev, "Obshchechelovecheskoe i klassovoe v mirovoi politike."
80. *Kommunist,* No. 17, 1988, in FBIS February 3, 1989; and his Lenin birthday speech, *Pravda,* April 21, 1989, in FBIS April 24, 1989.
81. Adamishin, "Humanity's Common Destiny," *International Affairs,* No. 2, 1989, p. 9.
82. Sergei Vasilevich Pronin, "Ideologiia vo vzaimosviazannom mire," *Mirovaia Ekonomika i Mezhdunarodnye Otnosheniia,* No. 10, 1988, pp. 5–15. This article was introduced as a contribution to a discussion on the relationships of ideologies during a time of cooperative relationships with capitalist societies. The editors referred to the "evident need" to overcome some "outdated stereotypical propositions" about ideological struggle left over from the Brezhnev period.
83. Gorbachev to a meeting of representatives of parties and movements, November 4, 1987, in FBIS November 4, 1987. (Extracted in Document No. 3, Part Two.)
84. Georgi Mirski, *Pravda,* January 25, 1989, in FBIS January 26, 1989.
85. Ye. Plimak, in *Pravda,* Nov. 14, 1986, in CDSP, Vol. 38, No. 46, p. 10.
86. A. Bovin, *Izvestiia,* July 11, 1987, in CDSP, Vol. 39, No. 28, p. 6.
87. Yuri Afanasyev, *Literaturnaia Rossiia,* June 17, 1988, in JPRS-UPA, August 16, 1988. See also G. Diligenskii, "Revoliutsionnaia teoria i sovremennost'," *Mirovaia Ekonomika i Mezhdunarodnye Otnosheniia,* No. 3, 1988, pp. 15–26, esp. pp. 15–16 (also in JPRS-UIA-88-014, August 24, 1988). Diligenskii's views are described as "diskussionyi." He makes the point that circumstances have changed so much that "far from all" of Marxism-Leninism's propositions are still valid.
88. Diligenskii, *Revoliutsionnaia teoriia i sovremennost',"* p. 20.
89. Aleksandr Bovin interview in the Vienna *Kurier,* September 22, 1988, in FBIS September 22, 1988.

90. See Gorbachev's speeches to the January 1987, Central Committee Plenum, in FBIS January 28, 1987; the June 1987 Plenum, in FBIS June 26, 1987; the June 1988 party conference, in FBIS July 1, 1988; and *Pravda,* January 7, 1989, in FBIS January 9, 1989.

91. *Pravda,* January 7, 1989, in FBIS January 9, 1989; Moscow Television Service, January 21, 1989, in FBIS January 23, 1989; *Krasnaia Zvezda,* February 24, 1989, in FBIS February 24, 1989 (extracted in Document No. 10, Part Two); and speech at the Central Committee Plenum on agriculture, *Pravda,* March 16, 1989, in FBIS March 17, 1989.

92. Gorbachev Report to the Supreme Soviet, November 29, 1988, in FBIS November 30, 1988.

93. *Sovietskaia Rossiia,* March 13, 1988, in FBIS, March 16, 1988. (Extracted in Document No. 5, Part Two.) See Peter Reddaway, *New York Review,* August 18, 1988, for details on Andreyeva's links to Ligachev.

94. *Pravda,* April 5, 1988, in FBIS April 5, 1988. (Extracted in Document No. 6, Part Two.)

95. G. Diligenskii, "Mnenie redaktora: O pol'ze iasnosti," *Mirovaia Ekonomika i Mezhdunarodnye Otnosheniia,* No. 6, 1988. pp. 55–57.

96. Speech in Gorky, Tass, August 5, 1988, in FBIS August 5, 1988.

97. A. N. Yakovlev speech in Vilnius, Lithuania, *Pravda,* August 13, 1988, in FBIS August 17, 1988, pp. 30–31. Georgi Arbatov, another supporter of *perestroika,* charged rather nastily that only "sectarians and ignoramuses" fetishize class interests. (*Moscow News,* No. 39, October 2–9, 1988, in JPRS-UIA, October 28, 1988.)

98. See Gorbachev's speech to the Congress of People's Deputies, *Izvestiia,* May 31, 1989, in FBIS June 16, 1989. (Extracted in Document No. 11, Part Two.)

99. *Perestroika,* p. 217.

100. *Pravda,* November 3, 1987, in FBIS November 3, 1987. (Extracted in Document No. 2, Part Two.)

101. *Pravda,* May 27, 1988, in FBIS May 27, 1988. (Document No. 7, Part Two.)

102. Moscow Television Service, June 28, 1988, in FBIS June 29, 1988. (Extracted in Document No. 8, Part Two.)

103. Shevardnadze speech at the Ministry of Foreign Affairs, July 25, 1988, in *Vestnik Ministerstva Inostrannykh Del,* No 15, August, 1988, pp. 27–46 and also in *International Affairs,* No. 10, 1988, pp. 12–13.

104. Andrei Kozyrev, "Confidence and the Balance of Interests," *International Affairs,* No. 11, 1988, pp. 3–12.

105. S. Kondrashov on Moscow Television June 24, 1988, in FBIS June 27, 1988.

106. *Komsomol'skaia Pravda,* June 19, 1988, in FBIS June 20, 1988. Dashichev is a Department Head in the Academy of Sciences' Economics of the World Socialist System Institute.

107. "The Party Conference: A Foreign Policy Dimension," *International Affairs,* No. 8, 1988, pp. 65–70.

108. *Literaturnaia Gazeta,* May 18, 1988, in FBIS May 20, 1988, and *Komsomol'skaia Pravda,* June 19, 1988, in FBIS June 20, 1988.

109. *Literaturnaia Gazeta,* June 29, 1988, in FBIS June 30, 1988. Bogomolov was contradicted by Ambassador Lev Mendelevich, who was interviewed at the same time. Mendelevich insisted that Soviet security "was and still is, under a certain threat. We must always plan for the worst-case scenario."

110. See for instance *Perestroika,* pp. 150, 211.

111. *Vestnik Ministerstva Inostrannykh Del,* No 15, August 1988 and *International Affairs,* No. 10, 1988.

112. Gorbachev speech to the Ministry of Foreign Affairs in May 1986, in *Vestnik Ministerstva Inostrannykh Del,* No. 1, 1987, pp. 4-6, in FBIS September 2, 1987.

113. *Pravda,* September 30, 1987, in FBIS September 30, 1987; and *Pravda,* February 19, 1988, in FBIS February 19, 1988. (Extracted in Document No. 4, Part Two.) See also Y. Primakov, *Pravda,* July 9, 1987, in FBIS July 14, 1987, who noted that Soviet flexibility and concessions in the arms control negotiation process makes Western militarists uncomfortable.

114. Moscow Television Service, June 28, 1988, in FBIS June 29, 1988. (Extracted in Document No. 8, Part Two.) The term "feedback" also appears in Thesis No. 10.

115. *International Affairs,* No. 10, 1988, p. 19.

116. *Literaturnaia Gazeta,* May 18, 1988, in FBIS May 20, 1988, and *Komsomol'skaia Pravda,* June 19, 1988, in FBIS, June 20, 1988.

117. See Shevardnadze's speeches to the Ministry of Foreign Affairs in 1987 and 1988, *Vestnik Ministerstva Inostrannykh Del,* No. 2, 1987, in FBIS October 27, 1987; *International Affairs,* No. 10, 1988; and *Vestnik Ministerstva Inostrannykh Del,* No. 23, 1988 (summarized on Moscow World Service, in FBIS November 25, 1988).

118. Gorbachev speech to the United Nations, *Pravda,* December 8, 1988, in FBIS December 8, 1988. (Extracted in Document No. 9, Part Two.)

119. *Pravda,* February 19, 1988, in FBIS February 19, 1988. (Extracted in Document No. 4, Part Two.)

120. See Raymond L. Garthoff, "Mutual Deterrence and Strategic Arms Limitation in Soviet Policy," in Bernard F. Halloran, ed., *Essays on Arms Control and National Security,* (Washington, D.C.: U.S. Arms Control and Disarmament Agency, 1986), pp. 137-186.

121. *Pravda,* February 26, 1986, in FBIS February 28, 1986.

122. *Pravda,* September 30, 1987, in FBIS September 30, 1987.

123. *Pravda,* September 17, 1987, in FBIS September 17, 1987; also as "Reality and Guarantees for a Secure World," *International Affairs,* No. 11, 1987, p. 4. As Anatoli Adamishin recently put it: "The basic premise was that the more armed a state is the more reliably its security is ensured. The record has shown, however, that the expensive arms race is yielding the opposite result." (*International Affairs,* No. 2, 1989, p. 13.)

124. *Pravda,* February 26, 1986, in FBIS March 28, 1986 (extracted in Document No. 1, Part Two); and *Pravda,* September 17, 1987, in FBIS September 17, 1987.

125. May 8, 1985, in Gorbachev, *Selected Speeches and Articles*, p. 65.
126. Speech to June 1986 Central Committee plenum, in *ibid.*, p. 565.
127. Moscow Television Service, June 28, 1988, in FBIS June 29, 1988. (Extracted in Document No. 8, Part Two.)
128. June 1986 Plenum speech, in Gorbachev, *Selected Speeches and Articles*, p. 566; and *Perestroika*, p. 219.
129. May 8, 1985, Gorbachev, *Selected Speeches and Articles*, p. 67; *Pravda*, February 26, 1986, in FBIS March 28, 1986 (extracted in Document No. 1, Part Two); FBIS November 3, 1987 (extracted in Document No. 2, Part Two).
130. *Pravda*, February 19, 1988, in FBIS February 19, 1988. (Extracted in Document No. 4, Part Two.)
131. *Perestroika*, p. 149.
132. Speech to the June 1986 Plenum, in Gorbachev, *Selected Speeches and Articles*, p. 566.
133. *Perestroika*, p. 217.
134. *Time*, August 20, 1985; *Perestroika*, pp. 150-151; *Pravda*, February 19, 1988, in FBIS February 19, 1988 (extracted in Document No. 4, Part Two).
135. Moscow Television Service, June 28, 1988, in FBIS June 29, 1988 (extracted in Document No. 8, Part Two); see also Shevardnadze in *International Affairs*, No. 10, 1988, pp. 12-13.
136. See for instance, V. V. Zhurkin, S. A. Karaganov, and A. V. Kortunov, "Vyzovy bezopasnosti, starye i novye," *Kommunist*, No. 1, 1987, pp. 42-50; V. I. Dashichev, *Komsomol'skaia Pravda*, June 19, 1988, *FBIS* June 20, 1988; and S. Blagovolin, *Izvestiia*, November 18, 1988, in FBIS November 25, 1988.
137. See for example General M. Moiseiev, *Pravda*, March 13, 1989, in FBIS March 13, 1989.
138. *Pravda*, February 26, 1986, in FBIS March 28, 1986 (extracted in Document No. 1, Part Two); see also the June 1986 plenum speech, in Gorbachev, *Selected Speeches and Articles*, p. 566; *Perestroika*, pp. 219, 234; and FBIS November 3, 1987 (extracted in Document No. 2, Part Two).
139. *Time*, August 20, 1985; and *Perestroika*, p. 132.
140. Gorbachev speech to the USSR Ministry of Foreign Affairs in May 1986, in *Vestnik Ministerstva Inostrannykh Del SSSR*, No. 1, 1987, pp. 4-6, in FBIS September 2, 1987.
141. See the detailed review by Bruce Parrott, "Soviet National Security under Gorbachev," *Problems of Communism*, November/December, 1988, pp. 1-36.
142. *Pravda*, February 26, 1986, in FBIS March 28, 1986. (Extracted in Document No. 1, Part Two.)
143. *Pravda*, May 27, 1988, in FBIS May 27, 1988. (Document No. 7, Part Two.)
144. Moscow Television Service, June 28, 1988, in FBIS June 29, 1988. (Extracted in Document No. 8, Part Two.) In his speech to the Party Conference, Academician Yevgeni Primakov, head of the Institute for World Economics and International Affairs, said: "Only today are we beginning to ensure our security chiefly through political measures in the military sphere on the basis

of reasonable sufficiency. This means that in recent years alone, not forgetting for a second about the sacred cause of the security of the state, we are beginning to think about how to guarantee it using minimum resources, which we are being forced to divert from the development of the national economy and the enhancement of the prosperity of our people." (FBIS July 6, 1988.)

145. V. Zagladin, Moscow Radio June 24, 1988, in FBIS June 27, 1988.

146. *International Affairs,* No. 10, 1988. See also O. Bogomolev, *Literaturnaia Gazeta,* June 29, 1988, in FBIS June 30, 1988, p. 6; Anatoli Adamishin, *Pravda,* June 25, 1988, in FBIS August 30, 1988; and Anatoli Kovalev, "Soviet Foreign Policy Priorities," *International Affairs,* No. 10, 1988, p. 36. V. I. Dashichev also described heavy defense spending as a goal of the West: "We proclaimed the achievement of military-strategic parity between the USSR and the West to be an outstanding success of our foreign policy. However, it seems to me that, first, there was and there is no need for such parity and second, it also produced certain extremely disadvantageous results. . . . Taking advantage of our commitment to military parity, the United State and its allies have raised their ceiling and forced us to keep following suit." (FBIS June 20, 1988.)

147. FBIS December 8, 1988. (Extracted in Document No. 9, Part Two.)

148. FBIS January 9, 1989, and January 19, 1989.

149. *Krasnaia Zvezda,* February 24, 1989, in FBIS February 24, 1989. (Extracted in Document No. 10, Part Two.)

150. Gorbachev, *Selected Speeches and Articles,* p. 296.

151. *Pravda,* February 26, 1986, in FBIS March 28, 1986. (Extracted in Document No. 1, Part Two.)

152. *Pravda,* September 17, 1987, in FBIS September 17, 1987; identical to Gorbachev, "Reality and Guarantees for a Secure World," *International Affairs,* No. 11, 1987, pp. 3-10.

153. *Pravda,* February 19, 1988, in FBIS February 19, 1988. (Extracted in Document No. 4, Part Two.)

154. Moscow Television Service, June 28, 1988, in FBIS June 29, 1988. (Extracted in Document No. 8, Part Two.)

155. Gorbachev speech to the Trilateral Commission, TASS January 18, 1989, in FBIS January 19, 1989; and Gorbachev speech in Kiev, *Krasnaia Zvezda,* February 24, 1989, in FBIS February 24, 1989 (extracted in Document No. 10, Part Two).

156. See Leonid Ilyichev, "Policy Towards Developing Countries and Regional Conflicts," *International Affairs,* No. 10, 1988, pp. 49-50; Yevgeni Primakov, "USSR Policy on Regional Conflicts," *Ibid.,* No. 6, 1988, pp. 3-9; and A. Kolosovski, "Regional'nye konflikty i global'naia bezopasnost'," *Mirovaia Ekonomika i Mezhdunarodnye Otnosheniia,* No. 6, 1988, pp. 32-41.

157. *Perestroika,* p. 176.

158. Gorbachev speech at the 43rd UN General Assembly, *Pravda,* December 8, 1988, in FBIS, December 8, 1988.

159. Y. Plimak, *Pravda,* November 14, 1986, in CDSP, Vo. 38, No. 46, pp. 10-11.

160. *Pravda,* July 2, 1988, in FBIS July 6, 1988.

161. FBIS July 6, 1988.
162. *Komsomol'skaia Pravda,* June 19, 1988, in FBIS June 20, 1988.
163. Kozyrev, "Confidence and the Balance of Interests," *International Affairs,* No. 11, 1988, p. 8.
164. A. Vasiliev, *Izvestiia,* February 4, 1989, in FBIS February 9, 1989.
165. *Pravda,* June 16, 1983, p. 2.
166. See Brezhnev's report to the 26th Party Congress, *Pravda,* February 24, 1981, in CDSP Vol. 33, No. 8, p. 8.
167. Gorbachev report to the 27th Party Congress, *Pravda,* February 26, 1986, in FBIS March 28, 1986. (Extracted in Document No. 1, Part Two.)
168. *Perestroika,* pp. 171-89.
169. FBIS November 3, 1987. (Extracted in Document No. 2, Part Two.)
170. FBIS June 29, 1988.
171. See Sylvia Woodby, "The Death of a Dream? Gorbachevist Revisions of Marxism-Leninism for the Third World," presented to the Annual Meeting of the American Association for the Advancement of Slavic Studies, November, 1988; forthcoming in Sylvia Woodby and Alfred Evans, eds., *Restructuring Ideology in the Soviet Union: Gorbachev's New Thinking.*
172. *Pravda,* February 26, 1986, in FBIS March 28, 1986. (Extracted in Document No. 1, Part Two.)
173. See V. L. Sheinis, "The Developing Countries and the New Political Thinking," *Rabochii Klass i Sovremennyi Mir,* No. 4, 1987, pp. 77-90, in JPRS-UWC, December 9, 1987; G. Mirski, "K voprosu o vybore puti i orientatsii razvivaiushchikhsia stran," *Mirovaia Ekonomika i Mezhdunarodnye Otnosheniia,* No. 5, 1987, pp. 70-81; G. Mirski and V. Li, "Sotsialisticheskaia orientatsia v svete novogo politicheskogo myshleniia," *Azia i Afrika Segodnia,* No. 8, 1987, pp. 26-32; A. Kiva, "Socialist Orientation: Reality and Illusions," *International Affairs,* No. 7, 1988, pp. 78-86; and A. Kiva, "Sotsialisticheskaia orientatsiia: teoreticheskii potentsial' kontseptsii i prakticheskie realii," *Mirovaia Ekonomika i Mezhdunarodnye Otnosheniia,* No. 11, 1988, pp. 62-72.
174. A. Kiva, "Sotsialisticheskaia orientatsiia: teoreticheskii potentsial' kontseptsii i prakticheskie realii;" Kiva, "Socialist Orientation: Reality and Illusions;" and Mirski, "Sotsialisticheskaia orientatsiia v 'tret'em mire'." *Rabochii Klass i Sovremennyi Mir,* No. 4, 1988, pp. 118-129.
175. See Kiva, "Sotsialisticheskaia orientatsiia: teoreticheskii potentsial' kontseptsii i prakticheskie realii;" V. Maksimenko, "Politicheskoe zaveshchanie Lenina i nekotorye problemy sotsialisticheskoi orientatsii," *Azia i Afrika Segodnia,* No. 9, 1988, pp. 24-26; and I. Zevelev and N. Kara-Murza, "Protivorechiia obshchestvennogo progressa," *Azia i Afrika Segodnia,* No. 7, 1988, pp. 17-20.
176. Nodary Simonia, "Leninskaia kontseptsia perekhoda k sotsializmu i strany vostoka," *Azia i Afrika Segodnia,* No. 4, 1988, pp. 2-5.
177. Nodary Simonia, "Chestno vesti nauchnuiu diskussiu," *Azia i Afrika Segodnia,* No. 6, 1988, pp. 16-18.
178. Simonia, "Leninskaia kontseptsia perekhoda k sotsializmu i strany vostoka," p. 5; and Mirski, "Sotsialisticheskaia orientatsiia v 'tret'em mire'," p. 129.

179. Sheinis, "The Developing Countries and the New Political Thinking," p. 12.

180. *Vestnik Ministerstva Innostrannykh Del,* No. 22, 1988, pp. 12–17.

181. *Literaturnaia Gazeta,* May 18, 1988, in FBIS May 20, 1988; and *Komsomol'skaia Pravda,* June 19, 1988, in FBIS June 10, 1988.

182. *International Affairs,* No. 11, 1988, pp. 6, 7.

183. S. Agaev, "Political Realities of the Developing World and Social Dialectics," *Rabochii Klass i Sovremennyi Mir,* No. 6 1987, in JPRS-UWC, April 5, 1988, pp. 1–10; and A. Kaufman and R. Ul'ianovski, "K voprosu o sotsialisticheskoi orientatsii osvobodivshikhsia stran," *Azia i Afrika Segodnia,* No. 5, 1988, pp. 19–23.

184. Sheinis, "Capitalism, Socialism, and the Economic Mechanism of Modern Production," *Mirovaia Ekonomika i Mezhdunarodnye Otnosheniia,* No. 9, 1988, pp. 5–23.

185. M. Ponomarev, in *Krasnaia Zvezda,* July 8, 1988, in FBIS July 11, 1988.

186. Grigori Oganov, in *Sovetskaia Kul'tura,* June 23, 1988, in FBIS June 28, 1988. See also N. Kapchenko, "The CPSU's Foreign Policy Strategy and Today's World," *International Affairs,* No. 10, 1987, pp. 65–74.

187. See especially S. Sanakoyev, "Peaceful Coexistence in the Context of Military-Strategic Parity," *International Affairs,* No. 2, 1988, pp. 75–85, who gave a positive assessment of peaceful coexistence as practiced under all Soviet leaders, and asserted several times that the West has never chosen to accept coexistence with the socialist states, but has been compelled to do so.

188. Stephen Sestanovich, "Gorbachev's Foreign Policy: A Diplomacy of Decline," *Problems of Communism,* January/February, 1988, pp. 1–15.

PART TWO

Selections from Relevant Speeches and Documents

1. Political Report of the CPSU Central Committee to the 27th Congress of the Communist Party of the Soviet Union

MIKHAIL GORBACHEV

Pravda, February 26, 1986
in FBIS March 28, 1986

While duly commending the achievements, the leadership of the CPSU considers it to be its duty to tell the party and the people honestly and frankly about the deficiencies in our political and practical activities, the unfavorable tendencies in the economy and the social and spiritual sphere, and about the reasons for them. . . . The priority task is to overcome the negative factors in society's socioeconomic development as rapidly as possible, to impart to it the essential dynamism and acceleration, to draw to the maximum on the lessons of the past, so that the decisions we adopt for the future should be explicitly clear and responsible, and the concrete actions purposeful and effective.

The situation has come to a turning point not only in internal but also in external affairs. The changes in current world affairs are so deep-going and significant that they require reassessment and comprehensive analysis of all factors. The situation created by nuclear confrontation calls for new approaches, methods, and forms of relations between the different social systems, states and regions.

The arms race started by imperialism has resulted in the 20th century in world politics ending with the question of whether humanity will manage to elude the nuclear danger or if the policy of confrontation will take precedence, increasing the probability of nuclear conflict. The capitalist world has not abandoned the ideology and policy of hegemonism, its rulers have not yet lost the hope of taking social revenge, and continue to indulge themselves with illusions of superior strength. The sober view of what is going on is hewing its way forward with great difficulty through a dense thicket of prejudices and preconceptions in the thinking of the ruling class. But the complexity and acuteness of this moment in history makes it increasingly vital to outlaw nuclear weapons, destroy them and other weapons of mass annihilation completely, and improve international relations. . . .

The concrete economic and political situation we are in, and the particular period of the historical process that Soviet society and the whole world are going through require that the party and all its members display their creativity, their capacity for innovation and skill to transcend the framework of habitual but already outdated notions. . . .

Socialism sprang up and was built in countries that were far from economically and socially advanced at that time, differing greatly from one another in mode of life and their historical and national traditions. Each one of them advanced to the new social system along its own way, . . . The way was neither smooth nor simple. It was exceedingly difficult to raise backward or ruined economies, to teach millions of people to read and write, to provide them with a roof over their heads, with food and free medical aid. The very novelty of the social tasks, the ceaseless military, economic, political, and psychological pressure of imperialism, the need for tremendous efforts to ensure defense—all this could not fail to influence the course of events, their character, and the rate at which the socioeconomic programs and transformations were carried into effect. Nor were mistakes in politics, and various subjectivist deviations, avoided. . . .

It is quite obvious that the two socioeconomic systems differ substantially in their readiness and also in their capacity to conceptualize and resolve the arising problems. Such is the world we are living in on the threshold of the third millennium. It is a world full of hope, because people have never before been so amply equipped for the further development of civilization. But it is also a world overloaded with dangers and contradictions, prompting the thought that this is perhaps the most alarming period in history.

The first and most important group of contradictions in terms of humanity's future is connected with **the relations between countries of the two systems, the two formations.** These contradictions have a long history. Since the Great October Revolution in Russia and the split of the world on the social-class principle, fundamental distinctions have come to light in the assessment of current affairs and in the view concerning the world's social perspective. . . .

The difficulty that the ruling classes of the capitalist world have in understanding the realities, the periodical recurrence of attempts at resolving by force the whole group of contradictions dividing the two worlds are, of course, anything but accidental. Imperialism is prompted by its intrinsic mainsprings and very socioeconomic essence to translate the competition of the two systems into the language of military confrontation. By dint of its social nature, imperialism ceaselessly generates aggressive, adventurist policy. . . .

It was nothing but imperial ideology and policy, the wish to create the most unfavorable external conditions for socialism and for the USSR that prompted the start of the race of nuclear and other arms after 1945. . . .

Today, too, the right wing of the U.S. monopolistic bourgeoisie regards the stoking up of international tensions as something that justifies military allocations, claims to global supremacy, interference in the affairs of other states, and an offensive against the interests and rights of the American working people. No small role seems to be played by the calculation of using tension to exercise pressure on the allies, to make them completely obedient, to subordinate them to Washington's dictation.

The policy of total contention, of military confrontation, has no future. Flight into the past is no response to the challenges of the future. It is rather an act of despair which, however, does not make this posture any less dangerous. Washington's deeds will show when and to what extent it will understand this. We, for our part, are ready to do everything we can in order to radically improve the international situation. To achieve this, socialism need not renounce any of its principles or ideals. It has always stood for, and continues to stand for, the peaceful coexistence of states belonging to different social systems.

As distinct from imperialism, which is trying to halt the course of history by force, to regain what it had in the past, socialism has never, of its own free will, related its future to any military solution of international problems. . . . We are firmly convinced that encouraging revolutions from outside, and doubly so by military means, is futile and inadmissable. . . .

The myth of a Soviet or communist "threat" that is being circulated today, is meant to justify the arms race and the imperialist countries' own aggressiveness. But it is becoming increasingly clear that the path of war can yield no sensible solutions, either international or domestic. The clash and the struggle between the opposite approaches to the long-term prospects for world development have become especially complex in nature. Now that the world has huge nuclear stockpiles and the only thing experts argue about is how many times or dozens of times humanity can be destroyed, it is high time to begin a practical withdrawal from balancing on the brink of war, from an equilibrium of fear, to normal, civilized forms of relations between the states of the two systems.

In the years to come, the main struggle will evidently center on the actual content of the policy that can safeguard peace. It will be a complicated and many-sided struggle, because we are dealing with a society whose leading circles refuse to assess the realities of the world and its perspectives in sober terms, or to draw serious conclusions from their own experience and that of others. All this is an indication of the wear and tear suffered by its internal systems of immunity, of its social senility, which reduces the probability of far-reaching changes in the policy of the dominant forces and augments its degree of recklessness.

That is why it is not easy at all, in the current circumstances, to predict the future of the relations between the socialist and the capitalist countries, the USSR and the United States. The decisive factors here will be the correlation of forces on the world scene, the growth and activity of the peace potential, and its capability of effectively repulsing the threat of nuclear war. Much will depend too, on the degree of realism that Western ruling circles will show in assessing the situation. But it is unfortunate when not only the eyes but also the souls of politicians are blind. With nuclear war being totally unacceptable, peaceful coexistence rather than confrontation of the systems should be the rule in interstate relations. . . .

The imperative condition for success in resolving the topical issues of international life is to reduce the time of search for political accords and to secure the swiftest possible transition to constructive actions.

We are perfectly well aware that not everything by far is within our power and that much will depend on the West, on its leaders' ability to see things in sober perspective at important crossroads of history. . . .

The U.S. ruling circles are clearly losing their realistic bearings in this far from simple period of history. Aggressive international behavior, increasing militarization of politics and thinking, contempt for the interests of others— all this is leading to an inevitable moral and political isolation of U.S. imperialism, widening the abyss between it and the rest of humanity. . . .

Will the ruling centers of the capitalist world manage to embark on the path of sober, constructive assessments of what is going on? The easiest thing is to say: maybe yes and maybe no. But history denies us the right to make such predictions. We cannot take "no" for an answer to the question: Will mankind survive or not? We say: The progress of society, the life of civilization, must and will continue.

We say this not only by dint of the optimism that is inherent in Communists, by dint of our faith in people's intelligence and common sense. We are realists and are perfectly aware that the two worlds are divided by very many things, and deeply divided, too. But we also see clearly that the need to resolve most vital problems affecting all humanity must prompt them to interaction, awakening humanity's heretofore unseen powers of self-preservation. And here is the stimulus for solutions commensurate with the realities of our time.

The course of history, of social progress, requires ever more insistently that there should be **constructive and creative interaction between states and peoples on the scale of the entire world.** Not only does it so require, but it also creates the requisite political, social and material premises for it.

Such interaction is essential in order to prevent nuclear catastrophe, in order that civilization could survive. It is essential in order that other worldwide problems that are growing more acute should also be resolved jointly in the interests of all concerned. The realistic dialectics of present-day development consist in a combination of competition and confrontation between the two systems and in a growing tendency towards interdependence of the countries of the world community. This is precisely the way, through the struggle of opposites, through arduous effort, groping in the dark to some extent, as it were, that the contradictory but **interdependent and in many ways integral world** is taking shape.

Communists have always been aware of the intrinsic complexity and contradictoriness of the paths of social progress. But at the center of these processes—and this is the chief distinction of the communist world outlook— there unfailingly stands man, his interests and cares. Human life, the possibilities for its comprehensive development, as Lenin stressed, is of the greatest value; the interests of social development rank above all else. That is what the CPSU takes its bearing from in its practical activity.

We proceed from the premise that the main direction of struggle in contemporary conditions is to create worthy, truly human material and spiritual conditions of life for all nations, to see to it that our planet should be habitable, and to deal with its riches rationally. Above all, to deal rationally with the chief value of all—with people and all their potentialities. That is exactly where we offer the capitalist system to compete with us in a setting of lasting peace.

. . .

Socialism unreservedly rejects war as a means of settling interstate political and economic differences and ideological disputes. Our ideal is a world without weapons and coercion, a world in which every people may choose its path of development and its way of life freely. This is an expression of the humanism of communist ideology and its moral values. That is why the struggle against the nuclear danger and the arms race and for maintaining and strengthening universal peace will remain in the future the main trend of the Party's activity in the world arena.

There is no alternative to this policy. This is even truer in a period of exacerbation in international affairs. Never, perhaps, in the postwar decades has the situation in the world been as explosive, and hence more difficult and unfavorable, as in the first half of the eighties. The right wing group which has come to power in the United States and its main fellow travellers in NATO have turned sharply away from detente to a military policy of force. They have armed themselves with doctrines which reject neighborliness and cooperation as principles of world development and as a political philosophy in international relations. The Washington administration has remained deaf to our calls to halt the arms race and make the situation more healthy. . . .

It is necessary to search for, find, and use even the smallest chance in order to break—while it is still possible—the trend of growing military danger. Realizing this, the CPSU Central Committee again analyzed the nature and scale of the nuclear threat at its April plenum and determined practical steps which could lead to an improvement in the situation. We based ourselves on the following principled considerations:

Firstly, the nature of today's weapons leaves no state any hope of defending itself with military-technical means alone—let's say, by creating a defense, even the most powerful. Ensuring security is more and more taking the form of a political task, and it can only be solved by political means. First and foremost the will to go along the path of disarmament is needed. Security cannot be built forever on a fear of retribution, that is, on the doctrine of "restraint or deterrent." To say nothing of the absurdity and immorality of a situation when the whole world becomes a nuclear hostage, these doctrines encourage the arms race which sooner or later is capable of getting out of control.

Secondly, security, when one speaks of relations between the Soviet Union and the United States, can only be universal if one considers international relations as a whole. The highest wisdom is not in only worrying about oneself, or all the more, about damaging the other side; it is necessary for all to feel that they are equally secure, because the terror and alarms of the nuclear age give rise to unpredictability in policy and specific actions. Taking the critical significance of the time factor into account is becoming very important. The emergence of new weapons systems for mass annihilation is steadfastly reducing the time and restricting the opportunities for adopting political decisions on issues of war and peace in the event of crises.

Thirdly, the United States and its military-industrial machine, which so far does not intend to slow its pace, remain the locomotive of militarism. . . .

Fourthly, the world is in the middle of a process of rapid change, and nobody is capable of preserving an eternal status quo in it. It consists of many dozens of states, each of which has its own, quite legitimate interests. All of them are without exception faced with a fundamental task; that of mastering the science and the art of behaving with restraint and circumspection in the international arena, living in a civilized way, that is, in conditions of correct international intercourse and cooperation, without turning a blind eye to social, political, and ideological contradictions. . . .

In a word, the contemporary world has become too small and fragile for wars and policies of force. It is impossible to save and preserve it unless a resolute and irrevocable break is made in the way of thinking and acting which for centuries was based on the acceptability and admissibility of wars and armed conflict. . . .

Continuity in foreign policy has nothing in common with the simple repetition of what has already been covered, especially in approaching problems which have mounted up. What is needed is particular accuracy in evaluating one's own possibilities, restraint, and the highest responsibility when making decisions. Firmness in upholding principles and positions is necessary, as is tactical flexibility and the readiness for mutually acceptable compromises—the aim being not confrontation but dialogue and mutual understanding. . . .

The Soviet program [for disarmament] has been enthusiastically taken up by millions of people. . . . But one should also take into account the reaction of the center of power, which holds the key to the success or failure of the disarmament talks. Of course, the U.S. ruling class, or to be more precise, its most egoistic groups tied up with the military-industrial complex, has different and clearly opposite aims from our own. . . .

2. 70th Revolutionary Anniversary Speech

MIKHAIL GORBACHEV

Moscow Television Service, November 2, 1987,
in FBIS November 3, 1987

During the brief years when Lenin was in charge of Soviet foreign policy, he not only worked out its starting principles but also showed how to implement them in a most unusual, drastically changing situation.

Indeed, contrary to initial expectations, the breaking of the weakest link of the capitalist system was not the final, decisive battle, but a beginning of a protracted and complex process. One of the greatest services rendered by the founder of the Soviet state was that he saw in good time the real prospects opening up for the new Russia as a result of the victorious end of the Civil War. As he conceived, the country succeeded in obtaining not only a breathing space, but also something much bigger, a new period of time when our main international existence within the network of capitalist states was one. Lenin decisively suggested the course of learning and getting to now how to coexist with them for a long time.

Counterbalancing left wing extremism, he found a basis for the possibility of states with different social systems to coexist peacefully. After the Civil War only one and one-half to two years were needed to bring the workers' and peasants' state out of foreign political isolation. Treaties with the neighboring countries and then with Germany in Rapallo were concluded. England, France, Italy, Sweden, and other capitalist states extended diplomatic recognition to the Soviet Republic. First steps were taken to establish equal relations with the states in the East: China, Turkey, Iran, and Afghanistan.

All this does not simply represent the initial victories of Leninist foreign policy and diplomacy; it was embarking on a fundamentally new international development. The cardinal direction of our foreign policy was laid, and we call it by rights the Leninist course for peace, mutually advantageous cooperation among states and friendship among peoples.

Of course, not all our subsequent foreign policy work consisted of successes and achievements alone. There were errors. It was not always and not everywhere, before and after World War II alike, that we succeeded in making use of the opportunities opening up. We were unable to make use of the enormous moral prestige with which the USSR emerged from the war to consolidate peaceloving, democratic forces and to stop the organizers of the Cold War.

Our reaction to the provocative actions of imperialism was not always adequate. Yes, some things could have been done better, and more effective action could have been taken. . . . To a decisive extent and precisely thanks to this, we succeeded in averting the unleashing of nuclear war. We did not allow imperialism to win the Cold War. Together with our allies, we inflicted a defeat on the imperialist strategy of rolling back socialism. Imperialism had to moderate its claims to world supremacy.

At the new stage, it is on the results of our own peace-loving policies that we have been able to rely, elaborating new approaches in the spirit of the new thinking. Lenin's conception of peaceful coexistence has of course undergone changes. In the beginning, it was justified primarily by the need to create the minimum external conditions for the construction of a new society in the country of the socialist revolution. But while being a continuation of the class policy of the victorious proletariat, peaceful coexistence has gone on, especially in the nuclear age, to become transformed into a condition for the survival of all mankind. The April 1985 plenum of the CPSU Central Committee also became a milestone in development of Leninist thought along this same avenue.

The 27th congress provided a new external economic conception in detailed form. Its point of departure, you will recall, is the following idea: Despite the profoundly contradictory nature of the modern world and fundamental differences of the states which comprise it, it is a mutually connected, mutually dependent, and forms a definite integral whole. This is brought about by internationalization of world economic links, the all-embracing nature of the scientific and technical revolution, fundamentally new role of the media and communications, condition of the planet's resources, overall ecological danger, and glaring social problems of the development world which affect everyone. But mainly it is brought about by the rise of the problem of mankind's survival, for the appearance and the threat of the use of nuclear weapons has placed a question mark over its very existence. Lenin's idea of the priority of interests of social development has thus acquired new sense and meaning.

The new thinking, with its criteria that are those of the whole of mankind, and its orientation upon reason and openness, has started to make its way in world affairs, destroying the stereotypes of anti-Sovietism and suspicion toward our initiatives and actions. Of course, if one is to measure it by the scale of the tasks which present-day mankind is faced with solving, in order to ensure survival, then only a very, very small amount has yet been done. But a start has been made, and the first signs of the changes are obvious. . . .

In this connection, we should first of all, again from the standpoint of our Leninist teaching and making use of its methodology, ask ourselves difficult questions. First—and this has to do with the nature of imperialism, in which the main military threat is rooted, as is well known—the nature of the social system cannot, of course, be changed by the influence of external conditions. But is it possible at the present phase of world development and at the new level of interdependence and integrity of the world to have an influence on this nature that would block its most dangerous manifestations? In other words, is it possible to count on the natural logic of an integral world, in which general human values are the main priority, being able to limit the range of destructive actions of the egocentric, narrow, class-based features of the capitalist system?

Here is the second question, and it is connected with the first. Is capitalism able to free itself of militarism? Can it function economically and develop without it? Concerning our invitation to the Western countries for programs to be prepared and compared on the reconversion of economies—that is to say, their transfer to a peaceful footing—is that not utopian?

The third question is: Can the capitalist system do without neocolonialism, one of the sources for its present life support? In other words, is that system able to function without its unequal exchange with the Third World, which is fraught with unpredictable consequences?

Along with this, there is a further question: How realistic are the hopes that an understanding of the catastrophic danger in which the world finds itself—and we know that such an understanding is penetrating even the topmost echelons of the ruling elite of the Western world—how realistic is it that this understanding will be carried over into practical policy?

After all, however strong the arguments of common sense might be, however developed the sense of responsibility might be, and however great the instinct of self-preservation might be, there are things that must in no way be underestimated and which are determined by economic and consequently class interests. In other words, it is a question of whether capitalism will be capable of adapting to the conditions of a non-nuclear and disarmed world, to the conditions of a new and just economic order, to conditions of an honest juxtaposition of the two worlds' spiritual values.

These questions are far from idle. The answers to them will determine how historical events in coming decades will unfold. It is enough to raise only these questions in order to see the full seriousness of the tasks. Life will provide the answers. The correctness of the program for a non-nuclear, secure world will be tested not only by the impeccable nature of its scientific foundations, but it will also be tested by the course of events, which is subject to influences from the most varied and new forces. . . .

So what are we counting on, knowing that we shall have to build a secure world together with the capitalist countries? The postwar period has provided evidence of a profound modification of contradictions which have determined the main processes in the world economy and politics. I have in mind, first and foremost, the fact that they have developed in a way that, in the past, inexorably led to war, to world wars between the capitalist states themselves. Now the situation is different. Not only the lessons of the last war, but also the fear of weakening itself in the face of socialism, which has become a world system, have prevented capitalism from taking its internal contradictions to the extreme. They have begun to involve themselves in a technology race against each other. They have discharged with the aid of neocolonialism, and a unique kind of new peaceful repartition of the world has taken place according to the same rule about capital that Lenin revealed: Whoever is the richest and strongest at any given moment gets the biggest share. A number of countries have begun easing economic tension by pumping resources into the military-industrial complex under the pretext of a Soviet threat. The transformations taking place in the technological and organizational basis of the capitalist economy have also helped to reconcile contradictions and balance interests.

But that is not all. If in the past, faced with the fascist menace, an alliance of socialist and capitalist states became possible, does not a definite lesson follow from this for the present day, when the entire world has come face to face with the menace of a nuclear disaster and need to ensure the safety of nuclear power engineering and overcoming the ecological danger? These are all completely real and acute problems, demanding not only that we be aware of them, but also that we seek practical solutions.

Further, is the capitalist economy capable of developing without militarization? Here, one is reminded of the economic miracles in Japan, West Germany, and Italy. . . .

There is yet another most important or even crucial circumstance: Socialism is an integral part of this world. Having started its history seventy years ago and then turning into a worldwide system, it has determined the aspect of the twentieth century. It is now embarking upon a new stage of its development, once again demonstrating the possibilities that are inherent in it. One can imagine, for example, what a great reserve of peaceful coexistence lies in restructuring the Soviet Union alone! By allowing us to attain world standards in all the most important economic indices, it will enable a vast and most rich country to join the universal division of labor and resources on a scale which has never been seen before. Its great scientific, technical, and production potential will become a considerably more important part of world economic relations. This will expand and strengthen, in a crucial way, the material base of the all-embracing system of peace and international security. This is, incidentally, another of the most important aspects of restructuring and the place reserved for it in the fate of modern civilization.

The class struggle and other manifestations of social contradictions will exert influence on the objective process in favor of peace. . . .

Thereby another new truth shines forth: constant choice is becoming increasingly characteristic of the movement of history at the end of the twentieth and beginning of the twenty-first century, but the rightness of that choice depends upon how and to what degree the interests and intentions of millions, hundreds of millions, are taken into account. From this the responsibility of politicians is derived. For a real policy can be such, only if this novelty of the time is taken into consideration. The human factor is now emerging at the political level, not as a remote and more or less elemental result of the life and activities of the masses of the people and their intentions. It is erupting into world affairs directly. Without an understanding of this, in other words, without new thinking based on present-day realities and the will of the peoples, policy becomes an unpredictable improvisation, which is risky both for a country itself and for others. There is no long-term support for such a policy.

These are the grounds for our optimistic view of the future and the prospects for the creation of an all-embracing international security system. Our position on defense issues is quite logically linked with this. As long as the danger of war remains and as long as social revenge-seeking remains the pivot of the strategy and militarist programs of the West, we shall continue in the future to do everything necessary to maintain our defensive power at a level that rules out a military superiority of imperialism over socialism. . . .

3. Speech to a Meeting of Representatives of Parties and Movements Participating in the Revolutionary Anniversary Celebrations

MIKHAIL GORBACHEV

Moscow Television Service, November 4, 1987,
in FBIS November 4, 1987

When the mighty revolutionary wave had subsided, Lenin understood earlier than the others the whole complexity of the movement toward those aims which the October Revolution, as it seemed to many, had brought so much closer. And his concept of the New Economic Policy [NEP] translated his idea of peaceful coexistence, or as he put it, living in peace together, from the initially only political, even diplomatic sphere, to the sphere of the fundamental laws of the era.

Later, it is true, it happened that other ideas gained the upper hand, but we have now finally overcome attempts to play cunning tricks with history, when, at times we proceeded not from what actually was the case, but what we wanted to see.

In the eighties the peculiarities of world development became clearly revealed; these had been accumulating and maturing over the entire post-war period. These are primarily the peculiarities of the nuclear age, which have brought to the forefront the problem of the very survival of mankind. Furthermore, these are the process of complication of world economic links, stimulated by the contemporary scientific and technical revolution; the intensification of the interdependence of the countries and peoples of the world; the coming into being of its integrity, in conditions of diversity and contradiction. This, finally, applies to the exacerbation of global problems, which challenge the very biological ability of man to adapt to the dangers, the pace, and the stresses of modern existence.

All of this highlights anew the content of the idea of peaceful coexistence, which demands from political movements a new analysis and reinterpretation of their tasks, the overcoming of the ideological schemes and stereotypes that have taken shape.

This is no easy matter. Nobody has any ready recipes. Nobody has hold of an Ariadne's thread which would help us find a way out of the labyrinth of today's contradictory world. In setting forth our concept of the new thinking, we are by no means laying claim to a monopoly on the truth. We are ourselves seeking and are inviting others jointly to seek, ways along which mankind might arrive at the twenty-first century across the minefield of our days, and arrive at a nuclear-free and nonviolent world. Of course, in the historic perspective, it is socialism—this is our conviction—that will make the decisive contribution to overcoming the critical points arising in the development of civilization. It is this system alone which potentially possesses the capability of having effective influence on the search for that Hegelian medium, that balance of interests, that will enable mankind to make a breakthrough to a fundamentally new, different level which is salvation for it.

The potential of socialism has not yet developed to the full, by far. In essence, a most profound social revolution is going on, with its origins in the October Revolution. But the duration, novelty and unevenness of it, the combination and coexistence of progressive moves and recessions, the interchange and interconnection of revolutionary and evolutionary processes, make any logical schemes composed according to old text books unviable.

The logic of the social movement of our epoch is becoming more and more apparent. The essence of it is in the material and spiritual self-discrediting of the exploitative society. Neither the negative moments in the history of socialism, nor whole libraries of those who deny Marxism, nor the sharpness and refinement of ideological polemics in the world have been able to refute the conclusion that there is an alternative to capitalism, and that the alternative is socialism.

However, variability in development remains. At every successive twist in the historical spiral, the forces of the world have the opportunity to remove the most dangerous contradictions at any given moment, and thus continue their domination. Such is what happened, for example, with capitalism's use of the scientific and technological revolution. . . .

The fact that real socialism, as far as its technological development is concerned, is still lagging behind capitalism, also impeded the passage to a new level of understanding of these processes. The prerequisites for overcoming this lagging behind are taking shape during the course of the revolutionary restructuring of socialist society, of its transition to a qualitatively new condition. But it is precisely this society of tomorrow that represents this higher type of socialism that will help those seeking a social alternative.

You may have noted that in the report delivered during the festive session, I spoke of two particularly dangerous manifestations of capitalist laws: militarization and the unequal exchange with the developing world. However, these are only possible with the aid of appropriate state policy—and this policy enjoys support; it enjoys support for as long as the fear of the Soviet military threat persists; for as long as people are firmly convinced that there exist superior national interests and that there exist those of secondary importance; that there are subjects of world politics and economics and that there are objects, that is, the neocolonialist sphere.

With all its international consequences, our restructuring is demolishing the fear of the Soviet military threat and militarism loses its political justification. . . .

We will not forego, not by one iota, the real values of socialism. On the contrary, we will enrich and develop them, ridding ourselves of all that which distorted the humanistic essence of our system. We are certainly not striving for our class enemy to fall in love with us; we do not need that at all. What we are counting on is that life will compel him to take realities into account and to become aware that we are all in the same boat and that we must behave in such a way that it does not capsize.

For socialism, both class interests, as a system, and general human interests are, so to speak, fused into one in this course. And for capitalism there is no other rational path than coexistence and competition. It is only by joint effort that we can weaken and eliminate the global danger of an ecological infarct. The problem has long since become an international one. . . .

Like much else in today's world, the communist movement needs renewal and qualitative changes. Now it is particularly important that it is not only a national but, in its very nature, an international force. Such a force is particularly needed by contemporary mankind. As far as the CPSU is concerned, it does not imagine its internal plans and deeds outside of the international context, and not, of course, outside of the correlation with the significance which they have or may have for our brothers in ideals and for progressive forces in general.

We ourselves felt strongly how, in the period of stagnation, the international impetus of socialism had lessened, so that restructuring in the USSR became vital from this point of view as well. We are fully aware of the significance of our work at the new stage, not only in the world economic and political context, but also in the context of moral support for the forces of socialism, democracy and progress. But mere parallel activities in our countries are insufficient. Cooperation is also necessary, but in contemporary forms of course. A more perfect standard, if one may put it like this, of mutual relations between progressive forces is required, such a standard which might make it possible to accumulate the whole diversity of experience, and help to understand the world surrounding us in all of its multitude of colors and contradiction.

The arrogance of a belief in one's omniscience is akin to fear of one's inability to master new problems; it bears witness to the tenacious habit of rejecting out of hand other points of view. Here you get neither dialogue nor productive discussion, but the main thing is that the cause suffers. Just as it was impossible in the beginning of the century to dogmatically extrapolate all of the tenets put forward by Marx and Engels for the age of imperialism, so still more it is impossible to carry out such an operation in assessing modern times with the aid of postulates which arose in the fifties, sixties, or even the thirties.

The theoretical legacy which our predecessors created in the name of man's social liberation must be read again in such a way as would make it possible to have a precise analysis of the new realities and to arrive at the optimally correct political conclusions. Many questions have to be answered in the search for a programmatic alternative to a society of antagonisms, and of confrontational tension in the world arena. . . .

4. Speech to the Central Committee Plenum

MIKHAIL GORBACHEV

Pravda, February 19, 1988,
in FBIS February 19, 1988

The Twenty-Seventh CPSU Congress provided a detailed interpretation of the philosophy of peaceful coexistence as we move from the old to the new century and validated the concept of an all-embracing system of peace and international security. Our initiatives in the disarmament sphere and other concrete steps in the international arena are now no longer improvisation, not simply a reaction to given Western political moves and actions as often happened before. They were given a firm, long-term scientific basis.

Thus the path was laid to Geneva, then to Reykjavik, and finally to Washington for the signing with the United States at summit level of the first nuclear weapons reduction agreement ever—the treaty on intermediate- and shorter-range missiles. I believe that when assessing its significance we all agree that it really does confirm the correctness of the policy begun by the April 1985 Plenum validated in theoretical and political terms at the twenty-seventh congress. We say that the treaty signed in Washington marks the beginning of real disarmament. We want it to be that way, and we will work to ensure that it continues.

But it is also the result of the efforts of the struggle by the socialist countries, other progressive and peace-loving states, mass social movements, the United Nations, and the Nonaligned Movement against the nuclear threat. It is the result of the activity, consolidation, and mutual understanding of outstanding scientists, cultural figures, clergymen. It is also the consequence of the sensible and effective stance taken by many politicians, representatives of the business world, and military circles.

In its way the treaty indicates the potential for peace that has now been attained. It also demonstrates that the new thinking is not only capturing people's minds but has already begun to influence world policy. The elaboration of the treaty provides instructive experience. It showed the fruitfulness of equal if difficult and strenuous talks in which mutual interests and concerns were scrupulously taken into account.

However, the signing of the treaty is not a pretext for complacency or smugness. . . . The U.S. Administration is keeping its word and defending the treaty. But at the same time it is giving the nod to extreme right-wingers in their anti-Soviet, anti-communist rhetoric, not only in words, but in definite militarist-style deeds on the same pretext of the "growing Soviet threat.". . .

The positive statements from high-ranking figures about our restructuring are again interspersed with waffle about the "expansion of communism" and warnings that it should not, allegedly, be forgotten "who we are dealing with" and that, since the present Soviet leadership is not about to change its system, this calls into question its "diplomacy of smiles." Again they are fussing about the senselessness of any talks with the USSR, since it allegedly "cannot be trusted" at all. A consolidation of reactionary and extreme anti-Soviet forces is under way. All manner of "analysts" and Kremlin-watchers make appalling recommendations to governments, poison the minds of the public, and try to scare them with the "catastrophic" consequences for the West if the disarmament process is continued. . . .

We know why they are worried. Not only because disarmament threatens the profits of the military-industrial complex and the income of those who make a good living out of it. But also because they are scared of a rebirth of the appeal of socialist ideas and an upsurge in the prestige of socialism as a society of working people. They are scared that there will again be growing sympathy for our country and that the Soviet Union will be "rediscovered." All this undermines the "enemy image" and, consequently, the ideological foundations of anti-Soviet and imperialist policy. Things that served the reactionaries so well over the last few decades are being destroyed. That is why the "right wing" is unhappy about the innovative and peace-loving policy of the USSR. That is why they want to halt the momentum of disarmament, which is picking up speed. We must see all this and take appropriate measures in our ideological work and propaganda.

Comrades! Steps toward the solution of the Afghan problem are another significant international event, in parallel with the treaty on intermediate- and shorter-range missiles, in the period since the preceding Central Committee plenum. For a long time now this problem has had a profound and direct effect on Soviet people's feelings and our entire society.

Following the CPSU Central Committee April (1985) Plenum, the Politburo conducted a hard and impartial analysis of the position and started even at that time to seek a way out of the situation. But the practical solution of problems which would allow us to unravel the main knots of this most complex regional conflict proved to be a far from simple matter. . . .

Of course, comrades, our involvement in the Afghan conflict is a highly complex problem touching on many aspects of what we have to overcome in the course of restructuring and the consistent transformation of the new thinking into practical policy. But the main point now is that the Politburo is acting on this issue, too, in strict conformity with the principled line of the Twenty-Seventh CPSU Congress.

Generally, it ought to be said that both the scientific elaboration of the problems of the new thinking and their ideological substantiation are still at their initial stage. There is plenty of work to be done here in an atmosphere of expanding *glasnost*. Soviet people display a natural desire to look into everything themselves, to gain a better understanding of what is happening, and even more so to become knowledgeable participants in the nationwide struggle against the danger of war and in international contacts.

This is precisely why all necessary conditions are being created for decisively raising the informative and intellectual standards of foreign policy propaganda and of explanatory work and comments on international issues. This is a very important sector of our ideological activity, because some people are somewhat confused in understanding the essence of the new thinking, just as they are about our ideas and changes on the domestic front. This is no wonder: The problems are rather important, they will only grow bigger, and a struggle is being waged around them. . . .

We have countered the militarist doctrine which underlies the policy of strength with the concept of "balance of interests" and mutual equal security. Our state interests do not run contrary to the interests of the peoples and the masses of working people in any other society. Unless peace is preserved there will be no progress at all, and it would be senseless to talk about anyone's interests outside the solution of this task. The struggle to exclude war from international politics is a struggle to save millions of lives, primarily the lives of working people who would suffer from any war before anybody else and more than anybody else. The establishment of normal, businesslike relations with states from the opposite system, apart from anything else, would shake anti-Sovietism and therefore anticommunism, thus diminishing reactionary pressure against democratic gains and aspirations.

The elimination of militarism—the question we have raised keenly and are approaching in a businesslike, realistic manner—not only helps to curb the most reactionary forces but also promises an increase in jobs everywhere. . . .

The complexities of world processes and the unpredictability of the shifts and turns of world politics, the dimensions and extraordinary nature of the peace offensive we have undertaken and which has met with unprecedented international response, the resistance of powerful forces which objectively have no interest in peaceful coexistence and, finally, the need to be understood correctly—all this raises not only our political but also our theoretical responsibility by an entire order of magnitude. The fundamental theoretical question currently facing both Marxists and their opponents is the question of combining class-based and general human principles in real world development and consequently in politics.

The report on the seventieth anniversary of October set forth principled provisions on this score. A fundamental problem was posed: Is it possible at the present stage, with the interdependence and homogeneity the world has achieved by the end of the twentieth century, to exert on the nature of imperialism influence of a kind which would block its most dangerous manifestations? The criteria have been outlined for the competition between different social systems as have the opportunities for their coexistence in forms which would rule out universal catastrophe. Our social science has begun to embark more boldly on an analysis of the features and basic signs of our era. . . .

The new thinking is the correct understanding of the new realities subjected to analysis by the method of materialist dialectics. . . .The central link of the new thinking is the new role of general human values. K. Marx and V. I. Lenin indicated their importance. These were not merely general considerations stemming from the humanitarian basis of their teaching. In stressing the importance of the processes of internationalization taking place in the world, our great teachers revealed the objective basis of general human values, dialectically uniting them with socioclass values. Now all this is becoming the pivotal line of practical policy. This demand on policy is conditioned by both the negative and the positive processes of the present-day era; on the one hand by the growth of the unprecedented dangers to the very existence of the human race and on the other by the increase in the role of the masses and the general democratic factor in internal state and world politics.

This also requires substantially different international relations. What relations precisely? What should be the initial and absolute principle in these relations? . . . This principle is the recognition of freedom of social and political choice by each people and each country. This way of putting the question also contains no trace of utopianism or illusions. We are very well aware that diplomatic courtesies and propaganda will not convince the West of the need to recognize this principle.

Of course, we must in no way belittle the importance of our goodwill, of the new style of our international activity, of our desire for frank and fruitful dialogue for the sake of attaining that minimum of trust possible between representatives of opposing social systems, of our sincere rejection of the ideologization of interstate relations, of our readiness for compromise on an equal basis, without detriment to anyone's security—in brief, everything characterizing Soviet foreign policy in the period of restructuring. . . .

The most important function, I would say the historical mission, of the forces of socialism, democracy, and progress, consists in expanding and consolidating realities and indeed creating new realities which would create an insuperable barrier to the forces of aggression and intervention.

We, the Soviet Union, are creating and consolidating these realities by our restructuring. I want to say once again that all our foreign policy achievements and the very business of preserving peace are rooted here—in the successes of restructuring, in our work, comrades. But it is important that all our people should also assimilate the reverse link: The success of restructuring is impossible without a foreign policy based on the new thinking. . . .

5. "I Cannot Waive Principles"

NINA ANDREYEVA

Letter to the Editor, *Sovetskaia Rossiia*,
March 13, 1988, in FBIS March 16, 1988

I decided to write this letter after lengthy deliberation. I am a chemist and I lecture at Leningrad's Lensovet Technology Institute. Like many others, I also look after a student group. Students nowadays, following the period of social apathy and intellectual dependence, are gradually being charged with the energy of revolutionary changes. Naturally, discussions develop. . . . It is, of course extremely gratifying that even "technicians" are keenly interested in theoretical problems of the social sciences. But I can neither accept nor agree with all too much of what has now appeared. Verbiage about "terrorism," "the people's political servility," "uninspired social vegetation," "our spiritual slavery," "universal fear," "dominance by boors in power,". . . These are often the only yarns used to weave the history of our country during the period of transition to socialism. It is, therefore, not surprising that nihilistic sentiments are intensifying among some students and there are instances of ideological confusion, loss of political bearings, and even ideological omnivorousness. At times you even hear claims that the time has come to take Communists to task for having allegedly "dehumanized" the country's life since 1917.

The Central Committee February Plenum emphasized again the insistent need to ensure that "young people are taught a class-based vision of the world and understanding of the links between universal and class interests. Including understanding of the class essence of the changes occurring in our country." Such a vision of history and of the present is incompatible with the political anecdotes, base gossip, and controversial fantasies which one often encounters today. . . .

I support the party call to uphold the honor and dignity of the trailblazers of socialism. I think that these are the party-class positions from which we must assess the historical role of all leaders of the party and the country, including Stalin. . . .

Long and frank conversations with young interlocutors lead us to the conclusions that the attacks on the state of the dictatorship of the proletariat and our country's leaders at the time have not only political, ideological and moral causes but also a social substratum. There are quite a few people interested in expanding the bridgehead for these attacks, and they are to be found not just on the other side of our borders. Along with professional anticommunists in the West who picked the supposedly democratic slogan of "anti-Stalinism" a long time ago, the offspring of the classes overthrown by the October Revolution, by no means all of whom have managed to forget the material and social losses incurred by their forebears, are still alive and prospering. One must add to them the spiritual heirs of Dan and Martov and other adherents of Russian social democracy, the spiritual followers of Trotskiy or Yagoda, and the offspring of NEP-men, basmachis, and kulaks with grudges against socialism. . . .

I was puzzled recently by the revelation by one of my students that the class struggle is supposedly an obsolete term, just like the leading role of the proletariat. It would be fine if she were the only one to claim this. A furious argument was generated, for example, by a respected academician's recent assertion that present-day relations between states from the two different socioeconomic systems apparently lack any class content. . . . What is happening today, does the international working class no longer oppose world capital as embodied in its state and political organs? . . .

The first and most swollen ideological current which has already manifested itself in the course of restructuring claims to offer a model of some sort of left-wing liberal intellectual socialism which allegedly expresses the most genuine humanism, "cleansed" of class accretions. Its champions counter proletarian collectivism with the "intrinsic value of the individual"—modernistic quests in the cultural sphere, God-seeking tendencies, technocratic idols, homilies to the "democratic" charms of contemporary capitalism, and kowtowing to its real and supposed achievements. Its spokesmen claim that what we have built is supposedly not proper socialism, and that apparently "an alliance between political leadership and progressive intelligentsia has been formed for the first time in history" only today. While millions of people on our planet are dying from starvation, epidemics, and military adventures by imperialism, they demand immediate formulation of a "legal code to protect animal rights," attribute an extraordinary and supernatural reason to nature, and claim that intelligence is not a social but a biological quality genetically transmitted from parents to children. Can you explain to me what all this means?

It is the champions of "left-wing liberal socialism" who shape the tendency toward falsifying the history of socialism. They try to make us believe that the country's past was nothing but mistakes and crimes, keeping silent about the greatest achievements of the past and the present. Claiming full possession of historical truth, they replace the sociopolitical criterion of society's development with scholastic ethical categories. I would very much like to know who and why needed to ensure that every prominent leader of the party Central Committee and the Soviet Government—once out of office—was compromised and discredited because of actual and alleged mistakes and errors committed when solving the most complex problems in the course of historical trailblazing? Where are the origins of this passion of ours to undermine the prestige and dignity of leaders of the world's first socialist country?

Another peculiarity of the views held by "left-wing liberals" is an overt or covert cosmopolitan tendency, some kind of non-national "internationalism." . . .

I am also convinced: Any denigration of the importance of historical consciousness produces a pacifist erosion of defense and patriotic consciousness, as well as a desire to categorize the slightest expressions of Great Russian national pride as manifestations of great power chauvinism. . . .

It seems to me that the question of the role and position of socialist ideology is extremely acute today. The authors of timeserving articles under the guise of moral and spiritual "cleansing" erode the dividing lines and criteria of scientific ideology, manipulate *glasnost'*, and foster nonsocialist pluralism, which objectively applies the brakes on restructuring in the public conscience. . . . Principles were not given to us as a gift, we have fought for them at crucial turning points in the fatherland's history.

6. "Principles of Restructuring: Revolutionary Nature of Thinking and Acting"

Pravda, April 5, 1988,
in FBIS April 5, 1988

The April (1985) Plenum of the party Central Committee initiated a new stage of social development aimed at the qualitative renewal of Soviet society and at restructuring.

On starting this essentially revolutionary work on an unprecedented scale, far from everyone involved in it was aware of the difficulties awaiting us on the chosen path. But one thing was clear: We could not live in the old way. The country had begun to lose momentum, unresolved problems were building up, elements of social corrosion had become apparent, and trends alien to socialism had emerged. All this had resulted in stagnation and precrisis phenomena. . . .

The conclusion of the party, the people, and of all who feel profoundly and sincerely for the country, for socialism, and for our common future was unanimous: There was no alternative to restructuring. We could reject or even defer restructuring only at very great cost both to our society's internal development and to the international positions of the Soviet state and socialism as a whole. . . .

Now that we have embarked on the second stage of restructuring, questions to which answers already seemed to have been given have once again become topical. They include, above all, this one—can we not get by without breaking things, without radical measures, can we not confine ourselves just to improving what was created earlier? In the process of restructuring do we not risk losing or destroying much of what has been created over the seven decades since Great October?

Many difficult, painful questions are being raised. *Glasnost'* has shown that the debate sometimes lacks political culture and the ability to listen to one another and to conduct a scientific analysis of social processes, or else it simply lacks knowledge and arguments.

And restructuring itself is frequently understood in different ways. For some people it is just another cosmetic repair job. Others have seen restructuring as an opportunity for some kind of "dismantling" of the whole system of socialism, and if this is so, then the whole path traveled since October is declared false, and the values and principles of socialism groundless. Yet others get carried away with radical phraseology, nurturing in themselves and others the illusion of skipping necessary stages.

Why do these questions arise, and what do they reflect? There are many reasons. Some people have not yet gotten to the bottom of what is happening. Some people are not fully aware of the seriousness of the situation which has taken shape. Some people do not doubt their own strength—and not only their own strength. Some people find it hard to part with mental laziness and tranquility and are unaccustomed to assuming the burden of responsibility for their actions. Some people have already managed to take fright at the scale of the transformations.

Such diversity of reactions to the practical business of restructuring is understandable, particularly if you take into account both the burden of former conservative habits and the complex and unaccustomed nature of the new problems concentrated in this brief, three-year stage. It is clear that it is necessary to further explain the ideas and aims of restructuring and the causes which gave rise to it, to investigate social processes collectively, and to separate the wheat from the chaff in both the old and the new. All this—we repeat—is normal and natural. The debate in society on all questions of our life is also natural. It is proceeding and will continue to develop. Its beneficial influence on social development is becoming increasingly noticeable. . . .

The debate itself and its nature and thrust attest to the democratization of our society. The diversity of judgments, assessments, and positions constitutes one of the most important signs of the times and attests to the socialist pluralism of opinions which really exists now.

But it is impossible not to notice a very specific dimension of this debate. It occasionally declares itself not in a desire to interpret what is happening and to investigate it nor in a wish to advance the cause but, on the contrary, to slow it down by shouting the usual incantations: "They are betraying ideals!" "abandoning principles!" "undermining foundations!"

I think that we are not just dealing here with sociopsychological phenomena. Such a stance has its roots in command and edict-based bureaucratic management methods. It is also bound up with the moral legacy of the time as well as naked pragmatic interests and considerations and the desire to defend one's own privileges—whether material, social, or spiritual—at any price.

It is an axiom of Marxism that ideas and interests are mutually linked categories. Any interest is expressed in certain ideas. Behind all ideas there is invariably a particular interest. Conservative opposition to restructuring is composed of the weight of custom and habitual thinking and action derived from the past and the belligerent, selfish interests of those accustomed to living at others' expense and reluctant to kick this habit. It is against those interests that restructuring is objectively aimed, for restructuring, like every revolution, is not just for something, it is also against something. It is against everything that impedes our living a better, cleaner, and fuller life, making more rapid progress, and paying the least price for the inevitable mistakes and miscalculations that occur along the new path. . . .

Some people have become mentally confused and perplexed. The launching of democratization, the rejection of edict and command-based methods of leadership and management, the expansion of *glasnost'* and the lifting of all manner of prohibitions and restrictions have generated apprehension. Are we not shaking the very foundations of socialism, revising the principles of Marxism-Leninism? . . .

"Don't rock the boat!" others say, intimidatingly. "You'll overturn and destroy socialism."

There are also those who bluntly propose stopping or else turning back altogether.

The long article "I Cannot Waive Principles" that appeared in the newspaper *Sovetskaia Rossiia* on March 13 was a reflection of such feelings. . . .

Whether the author wanted it or not, the article is primarily aimed at artificially setting off certain categories of Soviet people against one another. And precisely at the moment when the unity of creative forces—despite all the shades of opinion—is more necessary than ever and when such unity is the prime requirement of restructuring and an absolute necessity simply for normal life, work, and the constructive renewal of society. . . . Moreover, the article is unconstructive. . . .

It is evident that by no means everyone has clearly realized yet the dramatic nature of the situation the country found itself in by April 1985, a situation which today we rightfully describe as precrisis. It is evident that by no means everyone is fully aware yet that administrative edict methods are totally obsolete. It is time that anyone who is still placing hopes in these methods or in their modification understood that all this has already been tried, tried repeatedly at that, and failed to produce the desired results. Any ideas about the simplicity and effectiveness of these methods are nothing but an illusion without any historical justification.

So how is socialism to be "saved" today?

Should authoritarian methods and the practice of blind obedience and stifling of initiative be retained? Should we retain the system whereby bureaucratism, lack of control, corruption, bribery, and petty bourgeois degeneration flourished lavishly?

Or should we revert to the Leninist principles whose essence is democratism, social justice, economic accountability, and respect for the individual's honor, life and dignity? Do we have the right, in the face of the real difficulties and unsatisfied needs of the people, to adhere to the same old approaches which prevailed in the thirties and forties? Has not the time come to clearly differentiate between the essence of socialism and the historically restricted forms of its implementation? Has not the time come for a scientifically critical investigation of our history, primarily in order to change the world in which we are living and to learn harsh lessons for the future?

The item published by *Sovetskaia Rossiia* virtually advocates the first option. The second option is dictated by life, which also posed the demand for restructuring.

It is our ideological adversaries who are banking on identifying the essence of socialism with the old thinking, authoritarian methods, and retreat from the principles of socialism. Surely it is obvious that in this context the positions taken by home-grown "mourners of socialism" coincide with the positions of socialism's opponents abroad? Surely, by scraping the rust of bureaucratism off the values, ideals and principles of socialism and cleansing it of all that is inhuman, we are releasing the best constructive forces for the struggle for socialism, for our values and our ideals? Surely the struggle against conservative thinking and dogmatism is a struggle for these ideals, against their distortion, and simultaneously against lack of ideological discrimination and nihilism? After all, it is the blind, diehard, undoubting dogmatists, whose nervous system is used to functioning strictly according to an all or nothing principle, whereby everything is either harmonious and good or falling apart and bad, who are likely to end up in a state of dismay and hysteria. It is they, incapable of withstanding the "tension of contradictions" and having lost their customary material and spiritual comforts, who turn into extreme nihilists before anybody else. . . .

The past is vitally necessary for the present, for solving the tasks of restructuring. Life's objective demand—"More socialism!"—makes it incumbent upon us to investigate what we did yesterday and how we did it. What has to be rejected, what has to be retained. Which principles and values ought to be considered really socialist? And if today we are taking a critical look at our history, we are doing so only because we want a better and more complete idea of our path into the future. . . .

To keep silent about painful issues in our history means to disregard the truth and show disrespect for the memory of those innocent victims of illegality and arbitrariness. There is just one truth. What is needed is clarity, accuracy, and consistency as a moral guideline for the future. . . .

The best teacher of restructuring—the one to whom we should constantly listen—is life, and life is dialectical. We should constantly remember the words of Engels that there is nothing that has been unconditionally established once and for all as sacrosanct. It is this continual motion and the constant renewal of nature, society, and our thinking that is the point of departure and the initial, most cardinal principle in our thinking. . . .

7. Thesis No. 10, Issued by the Central Committee for the 19th All-Union Party Conference

Pravda, May 27, 1988,
in FBIS May 27, 1988

Restructuring in the USSR is a factor of international significance. While possessing an inner force of positive influence on the world, it needed a foreign policy that would properly express its humanist nature and demanded the democratization of our international links and a different position for the country in the worldwide division of labor.

A critical analysis of the past has shown that dogmatism and the subjectivist approach have also left a mark on our foreign policy. It was allowed to lag behind the fundamental changes in the world and new opportunities for reducing tension and for greater mutual understanding between peoples were not fully realized. In seeking strategic military parity, we did not always exploit opportunities in the past for safeguarding state security by political means and, as a result, allowed ourselves to be drawn into the arms race, which was bound to affect the country's socioeconomic development and its international status.

New thinking, consistently scientific and free from historically outdated stereotypes, was established as the foundation of foreign policy. It reflects the realities of the contemporary world—multifaceted and contradictory, with global threats to the very existence of the human race and, at the same time, with enormous potential for coexistence, cooperation, and the political solution of acute problems.

The new political thinking has made it possible to put forward a number of major ideas that have gripped the imagination of a troubled world. The chief ones are: a program for the stage-by-stage elimination of nuclear weapons by the year 2000, a system of all-embracing security, freedom of choice, balance of interests, a "common European home," restructuring of relations in the Asia-Pacific region, defense sufficiency and a doctrine of nonaggression, international economic security, strengthening of national and regional security by lowering the level of armaments, willingness to mutually terminate the presence of foreign forces and bases on foreign territories, confidence-building measures, and the idea of directly involving the authority of science in world politics.

This is our foreign policy credo. We have declared it without trying to impose any conditions or dogmas on anyone, but invite everyone to pool their ideas and conduct a joint quest, taking into account national and general human interests.

Thesis No. 10

In the disarmament sphere we have proposed far-reaching solutions and have displayed a willingness for profound compromises. This has made it possible to achieve such major breakthroughs in world politics at Geneva and, in particular, Reykjavik, which imparted real momentum to the negotiating process and had a substantial influence on the entire international climate.

The entire style of our foreign policy activity has radically changed. Dialogue has become a distinctive feature of it. The unprecedented abundance of contacts at Soviet leadership level with the outside world—from heads of state to ordinary citizens—has essentially meant a "rediscovery" of the Soviet Union. For us it means feedback, the chance to know and understand the world better and make our policy accordingly, and to promote the formation of modern, civilized international relations.

In the priority area of relations with the socialist countries, we, along with our friends, have begun in a comradely manner to clean away the accretions of formalism and ostentation and have actually linked the principles of equality, independence, and noninterference with objective reality—the diversity of national forms of socialist society. Our internationalist links are built on the basis of mutual benefit, a balance of interests, and common responsibility for the fate and prestige of socialism and for enhancing its role in world development.

During the years of restructuring, relations have improved or have been established for the first time with a large number of states—neighboring and very distant. And relations have not been spoiled with anyone.

Mutual relations have been placed on a new footing with such influential forces in the world process as communist, social democratic, and other political parties, the Nonaligned Movement, and intellectual circles personifying the authority of science and culture.

Events have demonstrated that the new political thinking has correctly reflected the pressing needs and imperatives of the modern world. It has given hope, it has paved the way for a radical qualitative change in human consciousness, and it is increasing the real weight of world public opinion.

The incorporation of new thinking in international politics has been marked by major practical results—the treaty on intermediate- and shorter-range missiles was concluded and the withdrawal of forces from Afghanistan began on the basis of the Geneva agreements.

The definite improvement of Soviet-American relations, as symbolized by the summit meetings, makes it possible to hope for a fundamental turn toward the elimination of the nuclear threat. The multilateral negotiating process which we have been actively stimulating is bringing a ban on chemical weapons closer and creating an opportunity for easing the dangerous confrontation between the two most powerful military alliances—NATO and the Warsaw Pact Organization—and cutting conventional armaments and armed forces in Europe.

We are not disregarding the militarist danger inherent in imperialism. This determines Soviet defense building, whose effectiveness must henceforth be ensured by primarily qualitative parameters with regard to both hardware and personnel. The influence of the realities of the modern world and the possible modifications of a number of objective factors that have given rise to war make it possible to think that the safeguarding of the security of states will increasingly move out of the sphere of the correlation of military potentials into the sphere of politics, the primacy of law, and common human morality in the fulfillment of international commitments.

The radical economic reform and the new approach to foreign economic ties have brought about the beginnings of the country's more effective inclusion in the world economy.

On the basis of the first three years of restructuring, the main question which concerns our people and all the peoples most of all—has it been possible to diminish the threat of war?—can undoubtedly be answered in the affirmative. The direct threat of a war involving the major powers has diminished. The international position of the Soviet Union has notably improved, and not through a building up of strength but by increasing trust in our country. The situation in the world has become more stable and predictable. The prospect of curbing the arms race with all its consequences—including the reduction of the burden of military spending—has become more realistic.

Possibilities are opening up for opposing the threat to peace on a broader social and political basis than before and creating the grounds for resolving mankind's global problems through the joint efforts of the world community. The CPSU will act vigorously and persistently for the sake of these goals.

8. Report of the Central Committee to the 19th All-Union Party Conference

MIKHAIL GORBACHEV

Moscow Television Service, June 28, 1988,
in FBIS June 29, 1988

Comrades, restructuring in the USSR has become a factor of world significance. The cardinal changes in our own house have also required new approaches to international affairs. In assessing Soviet foreign policy in the postwar period we do not forget that imperialism created around us and our allies an actual emergency situation. The Western military bloc led by the United States behaved with open aggression toward socialism. The military threat to us was constant. It has not been removed to this day. The Soviet Union, however, together with its allies, simply could not but react to this, as well as to the single-minded psychological war against socialist countries. Nonetheless, in learning lessons from the past it is impossible not to admit that the command-administrative methods did not bypass the foreign policy sphere either.

It even happened that decisions of major importance were made by a narrow circles of persons, without a collective, all-round examination and analysis, and sometimes without due consultation with our friends. This led to an inadequate reaction to international events and to the policies of other states, and even to erroneous decisions. Unfortunately, it was not always weighed up what one or another option for action would cost the people or what it could result in. In response to the nuclear challenge thrown down to us and to the whole socialist world, it was essential to achieve strategic parity with the United States. That was done.

However, having concentrated on the military aspect of confronting imperialism, we did not always use the huge sums and attention to ensure the state's security, to reduce tension in the mutual understanding among the peoples, or to take advantage of the political opportunities that opened up in connection with the fundamental changes occurring in the world. As a result, we allowed ourselves to be drawn into the arms race, which could not fail to have an effect on the country's socioeconomic development and on its international position. The arms race, moreover, was coming close to the critical point.

Against that background our traditional political and social activity in favor of peace and disarmament began to become less convincing. To put it more pointedly, if this development had not been restrained by logic, we could indeed have found ourselves on the brink of a military confrontation. This is why not simply an improvement in foreign policy was needed, but a decisive renewal of it.

For that a new type of political thinking was required. The foundation for this was laid at the 27th party congress. It provided our international activity, in the context of restructuring, with a new philosophical basis. The new thinking is not a closed and completed doctrine. It is dialectical. It allows policies to be constantly improved and developed in keeping with the course of real life. And this, of course, is in keeping with our socialist choice, with Leninist principles. In the same way, in internal affairs the Soviet leadership turned to Lenin, to his experience: everywhere, in any situation to act from a position of realism.

Only a policy like that can effectively serve restructuring. Only in that case can it count on a realistic attitude on the part of those to whom it is addressed. Only in this capacity does it acquire the ability to assist in saving the world from impending thrusts. In analyzing the world today we have formed a clearer idea that international relations, without losing their class nature, are being increasingly realized as relations among people. We have taken into account the greater role in world affairs of peoples, nations, and the new national formations that are emerging. Given that situation in international affairs, one cannot fail to take into account the variety of interests. Taking them into account is an important element in new political thinking.

The growing nuclear threat and the increasing aggravation of other global problems are typical of the modern era. The increasing internationalization of all processes in the world is becoming increasingly integral and interconnected, despite its contradictory nature. We have tried to interpret in greater depth the idea initially founded in Marxism of the interconnection of the proletarian and class interest with that common to all mankind.

This has led us to a conclusion on the priority of values common to all mankind in our age. This is where the core of the new political thinking lies. It has allowed us to evaluate on a larger scale the vital significance, for contemporary international relations, of moral values, which have over the course of centuries been worked out by peoples and pooled and elaborated by the great minds of mankind.

In analyzing the fundamental changes in the world, many stereotypes that have fettered our potential and have, to a certain extent, provided opportunities to those who were engaged in distorting our real intentions are being overcome. A major role was played by our moving out to broad contacts with representatives of other countries, from heads of state and government to ordinary citizens, with generally acknowledged authorities in science and culture, with outstanding writers, with leaders and delegations of political parties, voluntary organizations and movements, with trade union and social democratic leaders, and with religious figures and parliamentarians.

Such a richness of direct communication, as it were, reopens the Soviet Union to the outside world. Ad we, for our part have received the possibility of better seeing and understanding the surrounding world, taking part in discussion of its problems and in the search for an approach to resolving them, deriving what is useful from ideas stemming from other cultures and spiritual traditions, which found expression, for example, in the Delhi Declaration of 1986. With the aid of this feedback, it has become easier to find mutual understanding on the significance of such values as freedom and democracy. All this has provided Soviet foreign policy with dynamism and has made it possible to advance a whole number of major initiatives.

These include the program for the phased elimination of nuclear weapons by the year 2000, the system for general security, freedom of choice, balance of interests, the common European home, restructuring of relations in the Asia-Pacific region, defense sufficiency and the doctrine of nonaggression, the reduction of the level of armaments as a path to the strengthening of national and regional security, the recall of troops and bases form other people's territories, confidence-building measures, international economic security, and the idea of directly involving the authority of science in world politics. Dialogue, and—in the sphere of disarmament—a readiness for deep mutual control are at the heart of our contacts through interstate channels.

This has made it possible to extend the range of trust far beyond the boundaries of the normal world outlook. We have discovered considerable potential for mutual understanding and a readiness for coexistence and cooperation, even in influential circles that are very far from us ideologically. Our sincere open invitations to engage in joint thinking and quests have received a great response throughout the world.

Glasnost and restructuring are imparting material persuasiveness to our foreign policy ideas and initiatives. This approach has made possible major breakthroughs in world politics, above all in disarmament, such as at Geneva and Reykjavik, which provided real movement to the negotiating process and predetermined the success of the summits in Washington and Moscow. As a result, the entire international situation is changing.

In the context of the new thinking there has been an examination of socialism's position in the world. Together with our friends, we have tried in a comradely way to free the internationalist essence of our relations from the accretions of the past. Personal contacts between leaders of parties and state have been revitalized and have become businesslike and frequent. Coordination of the socialist community's foreign policy is being perfected. World socialism is living through a difficult and crucial period. The attainment of new frontiers by the socialist countries and the revealing of their potential in national and international frameworks are raising the prestige and the role of socialism in world development.

A key place in the new thinking is occupied by the concept of free choice. We are convinced of the universality of this principle for international relations, when the very survival of civilization has become the main worldwide problem. This concept has been brought about by the unprecedented and growing diversity in the world. We are witnessing a phenomenon such as the active inclusion in world history of billions of people who for centuries remained outside its bounds. These billions of people are emerging on the stage of independent historical creativity in totally new conditions. In a setting of mounting national self-awareness everywhere, they will still have their say in seeking their own choice of path.

In this situation, the imposition from outside by any means—not to mention military means—of a social system, way of life, or policy constitutes the dangerous armor of past years. Sovereignty, independence, equal rights, and noninterference are becoming the generally acknowledged norms of international relations, which is in itself a major gain for the twentieth century. Resisting freedom of choice means placing yourself in opposition to the objective course of history itself. This is why the policy of force in all its forms and manifestations has historically outlived itself.

In a word, we are profoundly convinced that the new thinking and the policies based on it correctly reflect the pressing requirements and imperatives of the world today. They have revived hope and opened the way to qualitative changes in mankind's awareness. As the Central Committee Theses emphasize, we can give an unconditional yes in answer to the question that worries Soviet people most of all and on which they wish to hear an appraisal of the result of work over the three years: Has it been possible to remove the threat of war?

How is this expressed? It is expressed above all in the fact that the axis of international life is moving from confrontation to cooperation, mutual understanding, and talks with the prospects of reaching specific results, primarily regarding weapons of mass destruction.

Soviet-U.S. relations have improved. A treaty has been concluded to eliminate some nuclear arms. The all-European process has been revitalized at the interstate level, and particularly at that of the public. The Geneva accords and the withdrawal of our troops from Afghanistan, which has begun already, are important international landmarks in the matter of political settlements to regional conflicts, which are fraught with danger for the world as a whole and hold up the peoples' progress.

From the rostrum of our party conference, on behalf of the party and the people, may I once again express profound gratitude to the soldiers, officers, and civilians and all those whose fate has been touched and who have been hurt by this war. Our troops are leaving Afghanistan at the behest of the motherland which has shown wisdom, having over those years acquired new political and moral experience, a more profound understanding of the modern world, its contradictions and difficulties, on the way to the future.

All in all, comrades, an analysis of existing realities enables us to suppose that if it is possible to strengthen and develop these realities, then the world at the turn of the century will be determined by the following trends: gradual demilitarization and humanization of international relations, when reason, knowledge, and moral standards rather than egotistical striving and prejudices finally move states to resolve the many contradictions in the world and achieve a balance of interests, and when the right of everyone to freedom of choice is recognized. Guaranteeing the security of states will move more and more out of the sphere of the correlation of military potentials to that of political interaction and strict compliance with international obligations.

A comprehensive system of international security will be formed, chiefly by increasing the role and efficiency of the United Nations Organization. The colossal growth of scientific and technical potential will be exploited in a more civilized way for the joint good of all mankind and to solve global economic, ecological, power, food, medical and other problems. Varied and voluntary associations between independent states and peoples will mutually enrich them reliably, materially, and spiritually, and will strengthen the structure of universal peace.

Are there no illusions here? Have imperialist sources of aggression and wars really vanished? No. We are not forgetting the threat to peace from imperialist militarism and we believe that for the moment no guarantees have been provided for the irreversibility of the positive processes that have begun. The new political thinking allows precisely for the spotting and discovery of new opportunities for opposing the politics of force on a political basis that is wider than before. These opportunities are strengthened by new objective factors that have emerged in the second half of this century. It is this that determines our defense development, the efficiency of which must from now on be determined predominantly by qualitative parameters regarding both technology and military science and the makeup of the armed forces. It should ensure reliable security for the Soviet state and its allies and be implemented in strict accordance with our defense doctrine.

We will continue to look for ways to secure peace and international cooperation through our international political activity. Relations with the socialist countries will continue to be at the forefront in the future. We will consistently follow a policy of strengthening our relations with the developing countries and the Nonaligned Movement and have active dialogue and talks with state figures authorized by their countries, above all on the focus of world politics: disarmament.

During the years of restructuring, we have improved or set up relations for the first time with a large number of states, both neighboring and very distant, and with no one have we spoiled relations. We will try to act this way in the future as well. The CPSU regards itself as an inseparable part of the world communist movement, which is now conducting a difficult search for a way out onto a new stage in its historical development. Based on the foundations of full equality and respect, we will actively participate in this search. There is increasing international potential in our new relations with numerous public forces, representing world science and culture, with political parties and new ideological tendencies, above all with Socialists, Social Democrats, members of labor parties, and other so-called left-wing circles and movements. Our solidarity with the workers of the whole world, with those struggling against colonialism, racism, and reaction remains immutable. Comrades, notwithstanding certain mistakes and errors in the past, Soviet foreign policy as a whole has rendered great services to the country, to socialism, and to the whole of humanity.

Restructuring has demanded new qualities of it, both in essence and in form. Just as in domestic policy, it must in practice absorb the collective thought of the party and the people and directly take into consideration not only the changes under way, but also foreseeable ones. The objective processes in the world and our potential should become the subject of constant scientific and public discussion with the participation of the public and its organizations. The quality of information on international issues must be raised by an order of magnitude. . . .

9. Speech to the United Nations General Assembly

MIKHAIL GORBACHEV

Pravda, December 8, 1988, in FBIS December 8, 1988

Esteemed Mr. Chairman, esteemed Mr. Secretary General, esteemed delegates. We have arrived here to express our respect for the United Nations Organization, which is ever increasingly displaying its ability to be a unique international center in the service of peace and security. We have arrived here to express our respect for the dignity of this organization, capable of accumulating the collective reason and will of mankind. Events are increasingly confirming the world's need for such an organization. . . .

The Soviet Union's role in world affairs is well known, and taking into account the revolutionary restructuring that is taking place in our country, and which contains a colossal potential for peace and international cooperation, we are particularly interested in being understood correctly. Therefore, we are here to share our thoughts within the walls of this most prestigious world organization, and to let the organization be the first to learn about our new important decisions. . . .

Life is making us give up customary stereotypes, obsolete views, and free ourselves from illusions. The very concept of the character and criteria of progress is changing. It would be naive to think that it is possible to tackle the problems tormenting modern humanity with the aid of the means and methods which were used, or seemed suitable, before.

Yes, humanity has accumulated very rich experience in political, economic and social development in the most diverse conditions. But it derives from the practice and the make-up of the world which have already disappeared, or are already disappearing, into the past. Therein lies one of the signs of the crucial nature of the present stage of history. . . .

The history of the past centuries and millennia has been a history of almost ubiquitous wars, and sometimes desperate battles, leading to mutual destruction. They occurred in the clash of social and political interests and national hostility, be it from ideological or religious incompatibility. All that was the case, and even now many still claim that this past—which has not been overcome—is an immutable pattern. However, parallel with the process of wars, hostility, and alienation of peoples and countries, another process, just as objectively conditioned, was in motion and gaining force: The process of the emergence of a mutually connected and integral world.

Further world progress is now possible only through the search for a consensus of all mankind, in movement toward a new world order. We have arrived at a frontier at which uncontrolled spontaneity leads to a dead end. The world community must learn to shape and direct processes in such a way as to preserve civilization, to make it safe for all and more pleasant for normal life. . . .

Of course, radical and revolutionary changes are taking place and will continue to take place within individual countries and social structures. This has been and will continue to be the case, but our times are making corrections here, too. Internal transformational processes cannot achieve their national objectives merely by taking "courses parallel" with others without using the achievements of the surrounding world and the possibilities of equitable cooperation. In these conditions, interference in those internal processes with the aim of altering them according to someone else's prescription would be all the more destructive for the emergence of a peaceful order. In the past, differences often served as a factor in pulling away from one another. Now they are being given the opportunity to be a factor in mutual enrichment and attraction. Behind differences in social structure, in the way of life, and in the preference for certain values, stand interests. There is no getting away from that, but neither is there any getting away from the need to find a balance of interests within an international framework, which has become a condition for survival and progress. As you ponder all this, you come to the conclusion that if we wish to take account of the lessons of the past and the realities of the present, if we must reckon with the objective logic of world development, it is necessary to seek—and to seek jointly—an approach toward improving the international situation and building a new world. If that is so, then it is also worth agreeing on the fundamental and truly universal prerequisites and principles for such activities. It is evident, for example, that force and the threat of force can no longer be, and should not be instruments of foreign policy. This applies, in the first instance, to nuclear weapons, but it goes further than that. Everyone, and the strongest in the first instance, is required to restrict himself, and to exclude totally the use of external force. That is the first vital component of a nonviolent world as an ideal we declared, together with India, in the Delhi Declaration, and which we invite others to follow. Moreover, it is clear today that the stepping up of military force does not make any single power all-powerful. Moreover, a one-sided emphasis on military force, in the final analysis, weakens other components of national security.

The compelling necessity of the principle of **freedom of choice** is also clear to us. The failure to recognize this, to recognize it, is fraught with very dire consequences, consequences for world peace. Denying that right to the peoples, no matter what the pretext, no matter what words are used to conceal it, means infringing upon even the unstable balance that it has been possible to achieve.

Freedom of choice is a universal principle to which there should be no exceptions. We have not come to the conclusion of the immutability of this principle simply through good motives. We have been led to it through impartial analysis of the objective processes of our time. The **increasing varieties** of social development in different countries are becoming an ever more perceptible feature of these processes. This relates to both the capitalist and socialist systems. The variety of sociopolitical structures which has grown over the last decades from national liberation movements also demonstrates this. This objective fact presupposes respect for other people's views and stands, tolerance, a preparedness to see phenomena that are different as not necessarily bad or hostile, and an ability to learn to live side by side while remaining different and not agreeing with one another on every issue.

The self-assertion of the world's diversity makes attempts to look down on others and teach them "one's own" democracy untenable, not to mention the fact that democratic values "made for export" often lose their value very quickly. Thus, the question is of unity in diversity. If we state this in the political sphere, if we confirm that we adhere to freedom of choice, then the idea that certain people live on Earth by "divine will" while others are here purely by accident will be discarded. It is time to get rid of such complexes and to construct one's political line correspondingly. Then prospects for strengthening world unity also will open up.

The de-ideologization of interstate relations has become a demand of the new stage. We are not giving up our convictions, philosophy, or traditions. Neither are we calling on anyone else to give up theirs. Yet we are not going to shut ourselves up within the range of our values. That would lead to spiritual impoverishment, for it would mean renouncing so powerful a source of development as sharing all the original things created independently by each nation. In the course of such sharing, each should prove the advantages of his own system, his own way of life and values, but not through words or propaganda alone, but through real deeds as well. That is, indeed, an honest struggle of ideology, but it must not be carried over into mutual relations between states. Otherwise we simply will not be able to solve a single world problem; arrange broad, mutually advantageous and equitable cooperation between peoples; manage rationally the achievements of the scientific and technical revolution; transform world economic relations; protect the environment; overcome underdevelopment; or put an end to hunger, disease, illiteracy, and other mass ills. Finally, in that case, we will not manage to eliminate the nuclear threat and militarism.

Such are our reflections on the natural order of things in the world on the threshold of the twenty-first century. We are, of course, far from claiming to have the infallible truth, but having subjected the previous realities—realities that have arisen again—to strict analysis, we have come to the conclusion that it is by precisely such approaches that we must search jointly for a way to achieve the **supremacy of the common human idea** over the countless multiplicity of centrifugal forces, to preserve the vitality of a civilization that is possibly the only one in the universe.

Is there not here a certain romanticism, an exaggeration of the potential and maturity of public awareness in the world? We hear such doubts and questions both at home and from some of our Western partners. I am convinced that we are not losing touch with reality. Forces already have formed in the world which one way or another are inducing the **start of a period of peace.**

The peoples, broad circles of the public, really and earnestly want a change for the better in the state of affairs. They want to learn to cooperate. Sometimes it is even striking how strong this trend is. It is important for this sort of mood to begin to be transformed into policy. The change both in philosophical approaches and in political relations is an important prerequisite, providing a powerful spur to efforts directed at establishing new relations between states by relying on objective processes on a world scale. The corresponding conclusions are being made even by those politicians whose activity was at one time connected with the "cold war," sometimes at its most acute stages. From their experience of those times, they of all people, find it especially difficult to renounce stereotypes. And if even they are making such an about-turn, then it is obvious that with the coming of new generations, the possibilities will be greater still. . . .

The realities are now such that to have a dialogue which ensures the normal and constructive progress of the international process requires the constant, active participation of all countries and regions of the world, of those of great magnitude such as India, China, Japan, and Brazil, and of others, large, medium and small. . . .

Perhaps the term "restructuring" is not very suitable in this case. But I am, indeed, advocating **new international relations.** I am convinced that the times and the realities of the modern world demand that a stake is placed on the **internationalization** of dialogue and negotiating process. This is the **main generalizing conclusion** that we have reached from our study of world processes, which lately have been gathering strength, and from our participation in world politics. . . .

On January 15, 1986 the Soviet Union put forward, as is known, a program for building a nuclear-free world. Its embodiment in real negotiating positions has already provided material results. Tomorrow is the first anniversary of the signing of the treaty scrapping intermediate and shorter-range missiles. With still greater satisfaction, I say that the implementation of that treaty—the destruction of the missiles—is proceeding normally, in an atmosphere of trust and efficiency. It would seem that a breach has been made in the impenetrable wall of suspicion and hostility. Before our eyes we are seeing a new historic reality arising, **a turnaround from the principle of over-abundance of weaponry to the principle of reasonable sufficiency for defense.** We are present to see the first glimmers of the formation of a new model of ensuring security, not with the help of increasing weapons—as was almost always the case—but on the contrary through reducing them on the basis of compromise. The Soviet leadership has decided once again to demonstrate its readiness to strengthen this healthy process, not only in words, but in **deeds.**

Today I can inform you of the following: The Soviet Union has made a decision on reducing its armed forces. In the next two years, their numerical strength will be reduced by 500,000 persons, and the volume of conventional arms will also be cut considerably. These reductions will be made on a **unilateral basis,** unconnected with the negotiations on the mandate for the Vienna meeting. By agreement with our allies in the Warsaw Pact, we have made the decision to withdraw six tank divisions from the GDR, Czechoslovakia, and Hungary, and to disband them by 1991. Assault landing formations and units, and a number of others, including assault river-crossing forces, with their armaments and combat equipment, will also be withdrawn from the groups of Soviet forces situated in those countries. The Soviet forces situated in those countries will be cut by 50,000 persons, and their arms by 5,000 tanks. All remaining Soviet divisions on the territory of our allies will be reorganized. They will be given a different structure from today's which will become unambiguously defensive, after the removal of a large number of their tanks.

At the same time, we will also cut the numbers of the personnel of our forces and the quantity of arms in the European part of the USSR. Altogether, in that part of our country and on the territory of our European allies, the Soviet Armed Forces will be reduced by 10,000 tanks, 8,500 artillery systems, and 800 combat aircraft.

Over these two years we will substantially reduce the grouping of armed forces in the Asian part of the country, too. By agreement with the Government of the Mongolian People's Republic, a considerable part of the Soviet troops present there will return home. In adopting these decisions of fundamental importance, the Soviet leadership is voicing the will of a people engaged in an in-depth renewal of its entire socialist society. We will maintain our country's defense capability on a level of reasonable and reliable sufficiency, so that no one should find themselves tempted to infringe upon the security of the USSR and its allies. . . .

Relations between the Soviet Union and the United States of America span five and one-half decades. The world has changed, and so have the nature, role, and place of these relations in world politics. For too long they were built under the banner of confrontation, and sometimes of hostility, either open or concealed. But in the last few years, throughout the world people were able to heave a sigh of relief, thanks to the changes for the better in the substance and atmosphere of the relations between Moscow and Washington.

No one intends to underestimate the serious nature of the disagreements, and the difficulties of the problems which have not been settled. However, we have already graduated from the primary school of instruction in mutual understanding and in searching for solutions in our own and in the common interests. The USSR and the United States created the biggest nuclear missile arsenals, but after objectively recognizing their responsibility, they were able to be the first to conclude an agreement on the reduction and physical destruction of a proportion of these weapons, which threatened both themselves and everyone else. . . .

We are not inclined to oversimplify the situation in the world. Yes, the tendency toward disarmament has received a strong impetus, and this process is gaining its own momentum, but it has not become irreversible. Yes, the striving to give up confrontation in favor of dialogue and cooperation has made itself strongly felt, but it has by no means secured its position forever in the practice of international relations. Yes, the movement toward a nuclear-free and non-violent world is capable of fundamentally transforming the political and spiritual face of the planet, but only the very first steps have been taken. Moreover, in certain influential circles, they have been greeted with mistrust, and they are meeting resistance.

The inheritance and the inertia of the past are continuing to operate. Profound contradictions and the roots of many conflicts have not disappeared. The fundamental fact remains that the formation of the peaceful period will take place in conditions of the existence and rivalry of various socioeconomic and political systems. However, the meaning of our international efforts, and one of the key tenets of the new thinking, is precisely to impart to this rivalry the quality of sensible competition in conditions of respect of freedom of choice and a balance of interests. In this case it will even become useful and productive from the viewpoint of general world development; otherwise, if the main component remains the arms race, as it has been till now, rivalry will be fatal. Indeed, an ever greater number of people throughout the world, from the man in the street to leaders, are beginning to understand this. . . .

10. Speech to Kiev Workers

MIKHAIL GORBACHEV

Krasnaia Zvezda, February 24, 1989,
in FBIS February 24, 1989

In rendering account of ourselves to the people in the preelection campaign, we are right to note major positive changes in international activity. The threat of war has been weakened. The security of the Soviet Union has increased. The prestige of our policies has genuinely grown in the community of states and among the public. This is the main result of the international activity of our party and the Soviet Government from the point of view of the interests of the people and of every Soviet person.

When we had just embarked upon restructuring, the party leadership was primarily concerned as to how matters were proceeding at home, within the country, but then, having begun to restructure, we very soon realized the need to rethink the entire situation worldwide, or own position in the world, our relations with the socialist countries and with states of a different social system: the totality of international relations and problems. In this way we arrived at the new political thinking and a rejection of outmoded notions and patterns, of the habit of seeing the world in black and white and we realized at least two important things.

First, it is not possible to guarantee the security of one's own country without taking into account the security interests of other countries. In a nuclear age reliable security cannot be built by military means, no matter how excellent these might be from the point of view of technology. This prompted us to look again at the very concept of this security and to put forward a fundamentally new concept of comprehensive security embracing all aspects of relations between peoples and states, including their human dimension. Second, in the modern, interlinked and ever more integral world, progress is impossible in a society fenced off from the international process by sealed borders and ideological barriers. This is true of any society, socialist ones included. Genuine socialism, in which the system serves people rather than people serving the system, can develop fully only by interacting with the world as a whole and increasing its contribution in conditions equal with others—to the development of world civilization, receiving from this development all that does not contradict the principles from which it started. We must get involved in the world's political, economic, and spiritual life while remaining ourselves at the same time. At the end of the twentieth century, it is in this way alone that our motherland is able to get a second wind and to prove to itself and to others the efficiency, democracy, and humanity of the socialist system. These conclusions, which form the structure of the new thinking, prompted us to embark upon the definitive renewal of foreign policy.

We have decided on the maximal use of political opportunities to remove international tension, achieve mutual understanding with the West, and untie the intricate knots of international contradictions through dialogue, talks, and the search for reasonable compromises. This policy, firmly linked with the profound internal transformations in the country, has made it possible to shift such a boulder overhanging the world as the Soviet-U.S. confrontation. The improvement in relations between the USSR and the United States has created a turning-point in the whole world process. . . .

Comparing the present situation with what it was like just a few years ago, we can see the extent to which it has been transformed. Dialogues have come to be the norm. Despite all their complexity, negotiation processes produced major results for the first time when they initiated a real reduction in armaments, the settlement of regional conflicts, and a lasting improvement in the international climate.

Our troops have returned home from Afghanistan. The Soviet Union will proceed steadfastly along the path toward a political settlement of the situation in Afghanistan, calling on everyone, primarily the countries that signed the Geneva agreements, to act in a similar spirit.

One can legitimately regard as a gain for the new thinking the fact that the word trust has changed from a rather abstract category, mainly propagandist in quality, into a political term with specific content, and even into a criterion according to which the level of relations between states belonging to different systems and blocs has started to be measured.

At times we do not notice how the atmosphere is changing. After all, our relations with the West both in politics and in the public, scientific, information and propaganda spheres were basically revolving around the concept of the Soviet threat. They kept accusing and suspecting us and they did not believe a single word we said. Hostility and squabbling which poisoned the international atmosphere and which fanned the arms race were stoked up. Now there are only the inveterate retrogrades who continue to repeat the claims about the Soviet threat, although this does not mean that anti-Sovietism has been dropped from the arsenals by authors of military budgets, masters of the military-industrial complex, and by the ideologues of anticommunism. But the fear of the USSR, which has been whipped up for decades, has started to be dispelled in public opinion in the West. It is proving to be an ever decreasing burden for the serious-minded statesmen too. . . .

Our foreign policy, which is based on the principle of freedom of choice, de-ideologizing of interstate relations, balance of interests, and internationalization of many problems, is open to contacts and cooperation with the most varied forces of the present world. As it turns out, we are able to find a common language and the necessary modicum of mutual understanding with the representatives of such circles and such states with which, as it seemed, we could quite recently have nothing in common. . . .

Of course, a solution to the basic world problems still lies ahead. But there are also such problems to which we will still repeatedly need to seek approaches. But it is absolutely obvious—this is admitted by all serious-minded politicians—that the world has become more peaceful and safe. We can hear increasingly frequently from the most authoritative lips and from the NATO countries' state figures that the Cold War is receding into history. Surely all this is related to our security?

But an even more fundamental question arises. For the first time in the postwar years and maybe in all history our country's security has been strengthened not because of the escalation of military power and not because of the increase of the already huge defense expenditure. On the contrary, we have been able to begin the reexamination of our military doctrine in an unequivocally defensive spirit. We have embarked on a substantial reduction of our armed forces and armaments. We are cutting our military expenditure and have started a partial reconversion of military production, redesignating some of it to civilian needs.

Our foreign policy also serves the cause of restructuring in the sense that it clears the way for broader economic cooperation with the outside world and for the country to join in world economic processes.

We are making an abrupt change in our foreign economic activity, toward enabling the USSR to become a full participant in the international division of labor. We are ready to work with others, too, to establish a new world economic and political order which will serve as a reliable guarantee of the survival and development of civilization. We are experiencing a sort of boom in information, cultural, tourist, public and simply human ties with foreign countries and are thereby increasingly opening up to the world, and the world is increasingly opening up to us. This is a very important process, one objectively conditioned by the growing integrality of the world. But it is also a very complex process, for it is not a matter of borrowing whatever comes to hand so long as it is the most modern thing out; nor is it a matter of a cocktail of diverse values or, even more so, a matter of ingratiating oneself. What is involved is rather something so important for peace and progress as true knowledge about one another, interaction of cultures in an atmosphere of self-respect and mutual respect. Such are the chief components of the profound change for the better in the Soviet Union's position in the world, and they are all working toward the renewal of socialism.

In its turn, socialism itself is increasingly actively joining in the universal human process of historical construction. . . .

11. Report to the Congress of People's Deputies

MIKHAIL GORBACHEV

Izvestiia, May 31, 1989,
in FBIS June 16, 1989

Comrades, restructuring in the Soviet Union could not help being reflected in all our international activity, but it could not be implemented if the previous foreign policy were maintained.

The fundamental change in the foreign policy course is connected with the new political thinking that was gradually developed with the liberation from dogmatic ideas and from conclusions which were only correct in their own time and which had ceased to correspond to the realities of our days. New thinking is a dynamic concept which is continuing to develop and deepen, but its main starting point remains the conclusion of the 27th CPSU Congress about the lethal danger which nuclear weapons and the arms race present to mankind's existence, about the integrity and interdependence of the modern world, about the change in the nature of its contradictions, and about the substance of world progress.

At the basis of the new thinking lies a recognition of the priority of human interests and values, of generally accepted norms of morality as the obligatory criterion of all policy, freedom of sociopolitical choice which rules out interference in the affairs of any state and the need for de-ideologization of relations between states. Despite the profound differences between social systems, objective possibilities have appeared in each of them for moving on to a fundamentally new, peaceful period in the history of mankind.

In the reality around us there are any number of cases that do not, it appears, follow the direction taken by the new thinking. There are the forces of the past and contradictions inherited from the past. Thus we cannot renounce our army and say a farewell to arms. The same can be said of military alliances, the preservation of which depends not on us alone. But however necessary the old forms and means may still be, we must not allow them to block the new approaches to the construction of international relations. Therein lies the wisdom of all high politics, and therein lies the qualitative different of foreign policy in the period of restructuring.

We can now defend it by drawing on real results. Much has already become habitual and seems normal, but where would we be if everything had remained as before? The fever of international tension has abated. There is no direct threat of nuclear war. People of different countries have, as it were, looked each other in the face and realized how absurd enmity is. The reduction of nuclear arsenals has started. The Europeans have embarked on the lowering of the most dangerous military confrontation in the world. We have pulled our troops out of Afghanistan, and have started to withdraw them from the allied countries. The country has opened up to the outside world to take a fitting place in the international division of labor and enjoy its advantages. The restrictions and prejudices hampering our effective involvement in the tackling of global problems and scientific and cultural exchange have been removed.

Our foreign policy is turned to the whole world, but each instance naturally has its specifics and its special and important accents, both in a bilateral context and from the viewpoint of regional and international significance. This concerns the socialist countries in the first place. Mutual relations with them reflect a very crucial stage in the development of the socialist world. We sensed this in full measure during our visit to our great neighbor, the People's Republic of China, the normalization of relations with which was an event of worldwide importance.

There are and there can be difficulties in the formation of a new type of relations between socialist countries. But these difficulties can be overcome. The main condition here is mutual respect, noninterference in one another's affairs, friendly mutual understanding, profound interest in the experience of each other, the need for cooperation and the readiness for joint patient work. We have all this right now.

A major area of our foreign policy work is participation in the building of a 'common European home.' The fundamental ideas are well known. They have come into use in public opinion and negotiating practice. The foundations for healthy relations in the spirit of restructuring with all states participating in the Helsinki process have been laid and are gaining momentum. We will steadfastly continue the Vladivostok line in the Asian-Pacific region. The diversity of the tasks here is even greater. Both the 'agenda' and an amicable, constructive and respectful tone of relations have been determined with many countries. Here as everywhere we will continue to devote special attention to relations with countries. First and foremost this means the great India.

We all understand that Soviet-U.S. relations are of primary importance for world policy. We are ready to interact with the United States on a predictable and stable basis. We are ready to move forward combining continuity with fresh ideas.

We have discovered over these years extraordinary opportunities for closer and more productive ties with Latin America and Africa. Here too there are both common problems and specific features relating to individual states. Strengthening good neighborliness with all neighboring states remains of paramount concern to us.

The Congress of People's Deputies is to consider and legislatively approve the principles of our foreign policy course for the years ahead. I believe that the following should be involved:

The country's security should be maintained above all by political means as an integral part of universal and equal security, in the process of demilitarization, democratization and humanization of international relations, with reliance on the prestige and possibilities of the United nations. Nuclear weapons should be eliminated in the course of a negotiation process geared to disarmament and the reduction of the defense potential of states to the limits of reasonable sufficiency.

The use of force and the threat of force for the purposes of attaining any kind of political, economic or other goals are impermissible. In relations with other countries, respect for sovereignty, independence, and territorial integrity is immutable. Dialogue and negotiations oriented toward a balance of interests, not confrontation, should become the sole method of resolving international problems and settling conflicts. We are in favor of bringing the Soviet economy into the world economy on mutually advantageous and equal foundations and of active involvement in the formulation and observance of the rules of modern international division of labor, scientific and technical exchange and trade. We are in favor of cooperation with all who are prepared for it.

There is another fundamental matter. In the past our foreign policy practice in certain instances ran counter to the proclaimed exalted principles of socialist foreign policy. Arbitrary actions were carried out that caused serious harm to the country and had a negative impact on its international prestige. It was the consequence of the same command-based system and the secretive decision making that was characteristic of it. One of the important tasks of the political system as it is being reconstructed by us is to exclude such systems and methods. In the future all significant foreign policy decisions should be adopted only after they have been thoroughly discussed in the Supreme Soviet and its commissions, while the most major ones, for instance, those connected with allied relations and the conclusion of the most important treaties, should also be submitted for consideration by the Congress of People's Deputies.

The approval of the Congress of USSR People's Deputies for the aforesaid principles is not just of legal importance, but of immense political importance— both internationally and domestically.

Far from everyone in the West, comrades, believes that we have chosen this foreign policy course once and for all and that we do not intend to change it. And here in our country, too, not everyone yet understands the fundamental essence of foreign policy based upon the new thinking. Some people regard it as a sort of tactic, a temporary zig-zag or even a concession to the West. This—I want to stress, and I hope the congress will support this statement— this is our strategic policy which is profoundly well-grounded and which expresses the interests of the Soviet people and which, we are convinced, corresponds to the interests of all mankind. . . .

Index

ABM treaty. *See* Antiballistic Missile treaty
Accidental war, 42, 58
Administrative command system. *See* Command-administrative system
Afanasyev, Yuri, 8
Afghanistan
 invasion of, 14, 22, 36, 52, 119
 settlement of conflict in, 15, 46, 90, 106, 116
Africa Institute, 49
Agriculture, 10, 11
Andreyeva, Nina, 31, 32, 33
Andropov, Yuri, 49
Angola, 14, 15
Antiballistic Missile treaty (ABM), 41
Anti-Sovietism, 38, 82, 90, 91, 116
Arbatov, Georgi, 64(n43), 67(n97)
Armenia, 7
Arms control, 14, 15, 18, 40, 41, 61, 89. *See also* Arms reductions
Arms race, 17, 35, 36, 43, 44, 58, 75, 76, 103
Arms reductions, 42, 105, 116, 117
 conventional, 15, 41, 101, 112, 113
 nuclear, 15, 40, 41, 112, 113. *See also* Intermediate Nuclear Forces treaty
ASEAN. *See* Association of Southeast Asian Nations
Association of Southeast Asian Nations (ASEAN), 15, 50
Azerbaijan, 7

Balance of forces, 21, 58

Balance of interests, 23, 38, 49, 110, 114, 116, 120. *See also* National interests
Baltic peoples, 7
Bogomolov, Oleg, 37
Brest-Litovsk peace treaty, 22
Brezhnev, Leonid, 5, 6, 37, 55
Bush, George, 59

Cambodia. *See* Kampuchea
Capitalism, 29, 30. *See also* Imperialism
Capitalist militarism, 37, 42, 83, 84, 87, 91, 101, 107
Capitalist states, 21, 90
 and socialist states, 21, 84, 87, 90
 Soviet view of, 17, 29, 30, 42, 43, 76, 78, 82, 83
 See also Capitalism; Capitalist militarism; Imperialism
Central Committee of the Communist Party of the Soviet Union
 April 1985 plenum, 89, 90, 96
 commission on ideology, 9
 commission on international affairs, 33
 February 1988 plenum, 6, 11, 25, 31
 purge of, 9
 Theses for the 19th Party Conference, 35, 36, 37, 44
 Thesis No. 10, 50, 100–102
 See also Communist Party of the Soviet Union
CFE. *See* Conventional Forces in Europe

121

Chemical weapons, 36, 42, 45, 101
China, 15, 81, 119
Class interests, 24, 25, 33, 48, 84, 88, 91, 104. *See also* Class struggle; Human interests
Class struggle, 21, 22, 24, 26, 30, 32, 52, 57, 94. *See also* Class interests; Peaceful coexistence; Revolution
Cold War, 18, 35, 44, 59, 81, 92, 112, 117
Command-administrative system, 6, 8, 36, 97, 103, 120
Common European home, 105, 119
Common human values. *See* Human values
Communist Party of the Soviet Union (CPSU)
  19th Extraordinary Conference, 7, 12, 25, 36, 44, 46, 48, 50
  program (1961), 26, 27
  program (1986), 19, 20, 24, 27
  reform of, 6, 9
  27th Congress, 5, 19, 21, 44, 46, 49, 82
  See also Central Committee of the Communist Party of the Soviet Union
Comprehensive international security system, 15, 42, 89, 107
Confidence building measures, 41, 105
Congress of People's Deputies, 7, 39, 119, 120
Conventional arms control, 41. *See also* Arms control; Arms reductions; Conventional Forces in Europe
Conventional force reductions. *See* Arms reductions
Conventional Forces in Europe (CFE), 15, 41
Convergence, 22, 28, 57
Conversion of military production, 45
Cooperatives, 6, 10

Cost-effectiveness in foreign policy, 39, 44, 45
CPSU. *See* Communist Party of the Soviet Union
Cuba, 15, 51
Czechoslovakia, 45

Dashichev, Viacheslav I., 36, 37, 39, 48, 52
De-ideologizing history, 8
De-ideologizing interstate relations, 16–17, 18, 20, 23, 25, 29, 43, 51, 59, 92, 104, 111, 116
Delhi Declaration, 106, 110
Democratization
  of foreign policy, 39
  of Soviet domestic politics, 6, 7, 44, 97
Detente, 18, 19, 22, 37, 44, 48
Deterrence, 41, 79
Diplomacy of decline, 60
Dissidents, 15
Dogmatism, 8, 16, 35

East Europe, 7
East-West relations, 19, 21, 22. *See also* East-West tension; Peaceful coexistence; United States, Soviet relations with
East-West tension
  importance of reducing, 14, 15, 29, 46, 58, 60, 61, 76, 79
  and regional conflicts, 46, 47, 49
  Soviet responsibility for, 23, 35, 37
Economic competition, 10
Economic incentives, 10, 11
Economic reform, 6, 7, 9, 10, 102
Egalitarianism, 12. *See also* Levelling
Enemy image, 38, 43, 90
Escalation, 18, 46, 47, 60
Europe, 119
European Economic Community, 14

Feedback, 38, 101, 105
Foreign investment in the USSR, 15

Index

Foreign policy
 achievements of, 43, 101, 102, 105, 118, 119
 aims, 14, 15, 18, 19, 20, 23, 27, 29, 116, 119, 120
 and domestic policy, 5, 14, 36, 39, 44, 45, 92, 102
 errors of, 35, 36, 37, 38, 100, 105, 120. *See also* Self-criticism, of foreign policy
Foreign policy style, 38, 39, 101
Freedom of choice, 23, 50, 105, 110, 111, 114, 116

GDR. *See* German Democratic Republic
General human values. *See* Human interests; Humanism; Human values
Geneva. *See* United States-Soviet summits
Genoa conference, 22
Georgia (USSR), 7
German Democratic Republic (GDR), 45, 113
Glasnost' (openness), 6, 7, 31, 34, 36, 90, 96
Global issues, 16, 37, 78, 86, 96
Gorbachev, Mikhail
 assessments of, 50, 56, 57, 58, 59
 critique of predecessors, 36, 38
 evolution of, 5, 19, 20, 21, 29
 and foreign policy, 14, 19
 and ideology, 16, 17, 25, 55, 56
 lack of vision of, 12, 13, 59
 opposition to, 30, 31, 33, 34, 97
 power of, 7, 59
 pragmatism of, 8, 12, 56
 report to the 19th party conference, 12, 25, 36, 103–108
 report to the 27th party congress, 20, 21, 42, 75–80
 response to critics, 25, 31, 33
 70th revolutionary anniversary speech, 24, 29, 81–85
 speech to Central Committee plenum (February 1988), 5, 11, 25, 31, 89–92
 speech to 70th revolutionary anniversary celebration, 24, 50, 86–88
 speech to the United Nations (December 1988), 45, 109–114
 and the Third World, 50
 vulnerabilities of, 56, 57

History, revision of, 8, 94, 95, 99
Hitler, 26
Human interests, 24, 88, 91. *See also* Class interests; Humanism; Human values
Humanism, 20, 25, 28, 58, 78, 79. *See also* Human interests; Human values
Human rights, 14, 15, 16, 28, 42, 59
Human values
 and class values, 25, 27, 28, 33
 and foreign policy, 16, 25, 111
 and Marxism-Leninism, 78, 92
 and new thinking, 23, 104
 and the West, 59
 See also Class interests; Human interests; Humanism; Socialist values
Hungary, 4, 5, 7, 45

ICBM. *See* Intercontinental Ballistic Missile
Ideology
 and the arms race, 58
 and foreign policy, 27, 36, 55, 56, 57, 59
 functions of, 54
 and reform, 7, 8, 9
 and regional conflicts, 47
 revision of, 5, 7, 9, 11, 60, 88, 98
 and Soviet interests, 55, 60
 See also Leninism; Marxism-Leninism
Imperialism, 30, 91. *See also* Capitalism; Capitalist states
India, 110, 119

INF. *See* Intermediate Nuclear
 Forces treaty
Institute of Economics of the World
 Socialist System, 37
Intensive development, 5
Intercontinental Ballistic Missile
 (ICBM), 41
Interdependence of states, 20, 21, 52,
 78
Interests, 10, 11, 32, 97. *See also*
 Balance of interests; Class
 interests; National interests
Intermediate Nuclear Forces treaty
 (INF), 15, 41, 42, 43, 89
Intermediate range nuclear weapons,
 14, 15, 40. *See also* Arms
 reductions; Intermediate Nuclear
 Forces treaty
International economy, Soviet
 participation in, 14, 15, 102,
 115, 117
Iran, 15, 22
Iran-Iraq war, 15
Israel, 15

Japan, 15

Kampuchea, 14, 48
Khrushchev, Nikita, 26, 27, 38, 55
Kozyrev, Andrei, 52

League of Arab States, 50
Leasing of land, 6, 10, 11. *See also*
 Agriculture
Leninism
 and class interests, 24
 errors of, 30
 and human interests, 24, 78
 and new thinking, 6, 9, 10, 11, 104
 and peaceful coexistence, 24
 and *perestroika,* 8, 9, 10
 and Soviet foreign policy, 81
 See also Ideology; Marxism;
 Marxism-Leninism
Levelling, 11. *See also* Egalitarianism
Ligachev, Yegor, 31, 33, 62(n7)

Manichean imagery, 16, 54, 56, 59,
 116. *See also* Zero-sum thinking
Marx, Karl, 30, 91, 92
Marxism, 32, 33. *See also* Ideology;
 Leninism; Marxism-Leninism
Marxism-Leninism, 8, 11, 12, 13, 30,
 57, 58, 59, 60, 98. *See also*
 Ideology; Leninism; Marxism
Medvedev, Vadim, 9, 27, 28
Mendelevich, Lev, 68(n109)
Militarism. *See* Capitalist militarism
Military spending
 Soviet, 15, 19, 39, 44, 45, 46, 117
 United States, 44
Military threat
 Soviet, 29, 38, 77, 87, 90, 116
 Western, 37, 38, 103
Mirski, Georgi, 64(n43)
Modernization, 59
Mongolia, 15, 45, 51, 113
Moratorium on nuclear testing, 40

Namibia, 15
National interests
 and international relations, 22, 29,
 80, 91
 and Soviet foreign policy, 15, 18,
 35, 48. *See also* Balance of
 interests
Nationality problems, 7
National liberation movement, 25,
 47, 48, 50
National security
 as mutual security, 17, 79, 91
 policy, 42, 44, 45, 107, 115, 117
 See also Military spending;
 Military threat; Parity
NATO. *See* North Atlantic Treaty
 Organization
NEP. *See* New Economic Policy
New Economic Policy (NEP), 9, 10,
 86
New international economic order,
 42
New political thinking. *See* New
 thinking

Index

New thinking
  achievements of, 101, 106
  and arms control, 41, 42
  defined, 16, 23, 25, 82, 114
  evolution of, 17, 90, 104
  and foreign policy, 35, 43, 60, 100, 116, 118
  and ideology, 17, 92
  and nuclear war, 16, 42
  and priority for human values, 104, 118
  rationale for, 104, 106
  and regional conflicts, 47
  and rivalry between social systems, 114
  and Soviet society, 61
  and the Third World, 51, 52, 53
  See also Perestroika
Nicaragua, 14, 48
19th Extraordinary Party Conference. *See* Communist Party of the Soviet Union
Nonaligned Movement, 50, 89, 101, 107
Noncapitalist path to socialism, 51. *See also* Socialist oriented states
Non-offensive defense, 42, 113
North Atlantic Treaty Organization (NATO), 14, 15, 19, 40
Nuclear-free world, 75, 112, 113
Nuclear parity. *See* Parity
Nuclear testing. *See* Moratorium on nuclear testing
Nuclear war
  and de-ideologizing interstate relations, 17, 20, 22, 58
  and new thinking, 16, 42
  and peaceful coexistence, 19, 26, 27, 42
  and Soviet foreign policy, 27, 57, 59
  See also Escalation; Nuclear-free world; Peaceful coexistence

Openness. *See* Glasnost'
Opposition to Gorbachev. *See* Gorbachev, opposition to

Organization of African Unity, 50

Parity, 36, 42, 43, 70(n146), 100, 103
Party. *See* Communist Party of the Soviet Union
Patriotism, 95
Peaceful coexistence
  and class struggle, 22, 24, 26, 27, 30
  and East-West relations, 18, 77, 89
  and foreign policy, 81, 82, 86
  and nuclear war, 19, 26, 27, 42
  redefined, 19, 26, 27
  See also East-West tension; Nuclear war
Perestroika (restructuring), 6, 9, 11, 12, 13, 18, 31, 32, 33, 45, 48, 56, 57
  aims of, 6, 8, 57, 96
  and arms control, 18
  defended, 12, 13, 32, 33, 96, 98
  and foreign policy, 18, 48, 52, 92, 112, 114, 115
  and international relations, 112
  interpretations of, 56, 57
  and Marxism-Leninism, 9, 10, 11, 12, 98
  and military spending, 45
  reactions to, 11, 12, 31, 96, 97
  See also Economic reform; New thinking; Political reform
Perestroika: New Thinking for Our Country and the World, 20, 43, 50
Performance criteria, 10, 11
Pershing (missile), 36
Poland, 7
Political reform, 6, 7
Pragmatism, 8, 10
Primakov, Yevgeni, 48, 69(n144)
Program of the CPSU. *See* Communist Party of the Soviet Union

Rapallo treaty, 81
Razumovsky, G. P., 9
Reagan, Ronald, 29, 40, 41, 46

Reasonable sufficiency, 42, 70(n144), 113
Regional conflicts
  causes, 46, 50
  and East-West relations, 46, 47, 48, 49, 60, 61
  and Marxism-Leninism, 47
  settlement of, 116, 120
  and the United Nations, 46, 47
  See also Escalation
Restructuring. *See* Perestroika
Revolution, 20, 30, 37, 51
Reykjavik. *See* United States-Soviet summits

SALT II. *See* Strategic Arms Limitation Treaty II
SDI. *See* Strategic Defense Initiative
Secrecy, 38
Security. *See* National security
Self-criticism
  of foreign policy, 14, 35, 37, 43, 81, 100, 103, 105, 107, 120. *See also* Foreign policy, errors of
  of society, 5, 6, 13, 15, 75
70th revolutionary anniversary, 24
Shevardnadze, Eduard, 14, 15, 36, 37, 38, 39, 45, 52
Social conflict, 11
Socialism
  criteria of, 11, 12, 98, 99
  and humanism, 88
  prospects for, 30
  status, 13, 15, 87
  See also Socialist values
Socialism in one country, 54
Socialist oriented states, 49, 50, 51, 52. *See also* Third World states
Socialist values, 12, 13, 56, 88, 99. *See also* Socialism
South Korea, 15
Soviet image, 37, 38. *See also* Enemy image
SS-20, 36, 40
Stagnation (*zastoi*), 5, 6, 13, 88, 96
Stalin, 9, 31, 93
Stockholm, 41

Strategic Arms Limitation Treaty (SALT) II, 41
Strategic Defense Initiative (SDI), 19, 40, 41, 43, 44
Strategic parity. *See* Parity
Soviet threat, 29, 90, 116. *See also* Military threat
Supreme Soviet, 7, 39

Ten Commandments, 28
Third World socialism, 51, 52. *See also* Socialist oriented states
Third World states
  and the Soviet Union, 49, 50, 52
  and the West, 52, 53
  See also Regional conflicts; Socialist oriented states
Theses. *See under* Central Committee of the Communist Party of the Soviet Union
Thesis No. 10. *See under* Central Committee of the Communist Party of the Soviet Union
Turkey, 22
27th Congress of the Communist Party of the Soviet Union. *See* Communist Party of the Soviet Union

United Nations
  Gorbachev speech to, 25, 109-114
  and international security, 42, 120
  and regional conflicts, 46, 47
  Soviet attitude toward, 15, 109
United States
  militarism. *See* Capitalist militarism
  military aid, 14
  Soviet relations with, 18, 19, 29, 77, 106, 113, 116
  See also East-West tension
United States-Soviet summits
  Geneva (November 1985), 46, 107
  Reykjavik (November 1986), 41, 107
  Washington (December 1987), 41, 107

Index

See also Arms control; United States, Soviet relations with
Uzbekistan, 7

Verification, 41. *See also* Arms control
Vietnam, 15, 51

Warsaw Pact. *See* Warsaw Treaty Organization

Warsaw Treaty Organization, 15, 41, 45
Western encirclement, 60
World communist movement, 107
World revolution. *See* Revolution
World socialism, 105

Yakovlev, Aleksander, 33

Zastoi. See Stagnation
Zero-sum thinking, 17, 47, 49. *See also* Manichean imagery